Forever Wild:
The Adirondack Experience

In Celebration of the Centennial of the Adirondack Park

Katonah Museum of Art
November 17, 1991–January 26, 1992

The Hyde Collection
February 9–April 5, 1992

The New-York Historical Society
April 28–July 15, 1992

*The lands of the state, now owned or hereafter acquired, constituting the
Forest Preserve as now fixed by law, shall be forever kept as wild forest
lands. They shall not be leased, sold or exchanged, or be taken by any
corporation, public or private, nor shall the timber thereon be sold,
removed or destroyed.*

*Article XIV Section I
New York State Constitution*

Cover:
Charles Lanman
Untitled: Temporary Camp, n. d.
Oil on canvas
The Adirondack Museum, Blue Mountain
Lake, New York

The exhibition and the accompanying publication have been made possible by the generous support of
Mr. and Mrs. Frank Coyle
Mr. E. Kent Damon, Jr.
Mr. and Mrs. John Dillon
Mr. and Mrs. Ernest Ellison
Roger and Mary Doris Gilmartin and Family
Mr. and Mrs. Roy C. Turney
The Seymour H. Knox Foundation, Inc.
and the Exhibition Patrons and members of the Katonah Museum of Art.

Additional funding has been provided by public funds from the Westchester Art Fund of the Council for the Arts in Westchester, which is supported by corporate contributions and the County of Westchester.

The Katonah Museum of Art exhibition catalogues are supported in part by funds from the Ida and William Rosenthal Foundation.

Exhibition Coordinators: Ruth Dillon, Deborah McCain, Prudence Read
Docent Trainer: Anne Miller

Publication Design: Esther L. Clark
Publication preparation: Aline W. Benjamin and Naomi Brocki
Printer: Eastern Press
Typography: Lettra Graphics, Inc.
This publication has been printed in an edition of 1,500 and set in Simoncini Garamond

Exhibition Design: Arthur M. Clark

Publicity: Harrison Edwards, Inc.

Copyright 1991
Katonah Museum of Art
Route 22 at Jay Street
Katonah, New York 10536

ISBN: 915171-23-6
Library of Congress Catalog Card Number: 91-062653

Contents

Lenders to the Exhibition

Adirondack League Club, Old Forge, New York

The Adirondack Museum, Blue Mountain Lake, New York

American Antiquarian Society, Worcester, Massachusetts

Mr. and Mrs. Peter K. Bertine

The Benton Board, Canton Free Library, Canton, New York

Mr. and Mrs. Thomas Bissell

Hoagy Carmichael Collection, Croton Falls, New York

Sterling and Francine Clark Institute, Williamstown, Massachusetts

Mr. and Mrs. Thad Phillips Collum

Concord Free Library, Concord, Massachusetts

The Crandall Library, Glens Falls, New York

Mr. and Mrs. Anthony N. B. Garvan

Thomas Gilcrease Institute of American History and Art, Tulsa, Oklahoma

The Hyde Collection, Glens Falls, New York

Kent Collection, SUNY, Plattsburgh, New York

Munson-Williams-Proctor Institute Museum of Art, Utica, New York

The New-York Historical Society

Frederic Remington Art Museum, Ogdensburg, New York

Saranac Lake Free Library, Adirondack Collection, Saranac Lake, New York

The Gordon Stott Collection

Van Pelt Library, University of Pennsylvania

Milo and Ann Williams

Eleanor B. Wunderlich

John C. Wunderlich

Owen D. Young Library, St. Lawrence University, Canton, New York

Private Collection from an Adirondack camp

Private Collection from Kamp Kill Kare

Private Collectors

Foreword

The year 1992 marks the centennial anniversary of the official designation of the Adirondack State Park. Although the Park was certainly visited and explored before this designation, it is important to note, a century later, the significance and growth of its unique aesthetics. The exhibition, *Forever Wild: The Adirondack Experience*, examines the life and arts of this region beginning in the 1830s.

The Museum is especially grateful to Ruth and John Dillon, whose enthusiasm and first-hand knowledge of the Park and its diverse arts initiated and encouraged the project from the beginning. We are fortunate to have the participation and the scholarship of Anthony Garvan, Craig Gilborn, Paul Jamieson, Paul Malo, and Robert McGrath. We are indebted to those who have recognized the meaning of "Forever Wild" by providing generous support to the exhibition and its publication.

Additionally, the exhibition coordinators, Ruth Dillon, Deborah McCain, and Prudence Read, have all devoted their own generous time toward the project; without their diligence and devotion the presentation of this exhibition at the Museum, the Hyde Collection, and The New-York Historical Society would not have been possible.

George G. King
Director

Acknowledgements

Our thanks go first to The Adirondack Museum, its Director, Craig Gilborn, and its staff. The Museum has been our main source of inspiration as well as the repository of at least half the objects exhibited in "Forever Wild." We have been welcomed by the staff in fair and foul weather. They have given freely of their time and knowledge to answer our questions and show us their collections. In addition to Craig Gilborn, Caroline Welsh, Curator of Exhibitions; Tracy Meehan, Registrar; Jerold Pepper, Librarian; and Jim Meehan, Curatorial Assistant, have been our guides. Further valued help and advice were given by consultants Robert McGrath for the fine arts, Paul Malo for architecture, and Craig Gilborn for the decorative arts. We are grateful to five eminent authorities on the Adirondacks whose diverse voices add to our understanding and appreciation of our New York State treasure. The generosity of all our lenders has made possible a glimpse of the richness and complexity of the human responses to the Adirondacks.

The Katonah Museum of Art staff provided essential services with a maximum of good humor and Arthur Clark, as ever, has provided an evocative and original setting to present the Adirondack story.

Ruth Dillon
Deborah McCain
Anne Miller
Prudence Read
Exhibition Coordinators

Art of the Adirondacks

CRAIG GILBORN

The Adirondacks rise in the northeastern corner of New York. The region is like an inverted saucer, but oval in shape and extending roughly 120 miles north to south and 100 miles between Lake Champlain in the east and Boonville in the west, with elevations ranging from near sea level to the mile-high summit of Mt. Marcy. Rivers and streams tumble down the forested uplands and emerge on the cultivated glacial plateau of farms and towns that surround the Adirondacks everywhere except on Lake Champlain. Adirondack waters end up in the Atlantic; the headwaters of the Hudson originate in remote Lake-Tear-of-the-Clouds, some 315 miles north of Manhattan's skyscrapers.

The Adirondacks have been a source of natural resources to New York since late colonial times. Water, timber, ore, game, and recreation have been its chief products. The political entity called the Adirondack Park, established in 1892, is one of several milestones by which the state's citizens and lawmakers have attempted to protect the region from environmental abuses related to the logging industry and such practices as cutting trees and allowing the cutover lands to be sold at auction for unpaid taxes. This exhibition, organized by the Katonah Museum of Art, is occasioned by the 100th anniversary, in 1992, of the Adirondack Park.

The Adirondack Park occupies a fifth of New York's area and is itself larger in extent than seven states. But the Park's size, its proximity to urban population centers in the northeast, and the leadership role played by its advocates in the conservation movement in the United States are more a caricature than a portrait. Statistics about the Adirondacks, a staple of essays such as this one, skip over the contrary spirit of the place and the antic responses of people who do more than vacation here. Adirondackers can identify with the characters in the television series, "Northern Exposure." The eccentric behavior of these Alaskans is a reasonable response, they know, to confinement.

An instance is the genius of the region in frustrating developers who have pitted themselves and their fortunes against the scope and cycle of what is as near to being a wilderness as can be found on this side of the Mississippi River. Gone are most railroads; and those large enclaves of privilege, the so-called Great Camps, are literally shells of their old selves. Communities formerly sustained largely by company mines and mills are now relics of history. The Adirondacks have resisted outsized projects that aspired to tame and bring them to heel.

Life for the majority of Adirondackers is a matter of fundamentals and little extras; steady employment and adequate wages are visitors to fewer homes here than elsewhere in the state. But the region has always had a subsistence economy, and this experience has conditioned its people to look to the person and not his testimonials. In 1881 a minister from Philadelphia observed in *The Wilderness Cure*, a guide to Saranac Lake for prospective patients seeking recovery from tuberculosis, "The want of money here, while it may enhance its value as a personal possession, seems to give the native a supreme indifference to the wealth of others." Nature's eminence in the Adirondacks places its residents in an intimacy

Craig Gilborn is Director of The Adirondack Museum at Blue Mountain Lake, New York. A lecturer and author, he has written articles and books, among them *Adirondack Furniture and the Rustic Tradition,* 1987, and *Durant: The Fortunes and Woodlands Camps of a Family in the Adirondacks,* 1981.

with one another and their surroundings that is forced and chosen at the same time. "Like being in God's pocket" is what one elderly woman said of her girlhood in Indian Lake.

An understanding of Adirondack art begins with knowledge about the conditions of that art, which is the aim of this brief essay. Besides its maintenance economy and isolation, features of rural life wherever it may be found, a third component, the forest, must be added to the Adirondack equation. What water is to fish, the forest is to the culture of the Adirondacks.

The tree is the Adirondacker's chief resource and companion. His home is made with wood, and he knows it can always be warmed by it. Wood is a living for some and a source of pocket money for others. The collective memory of the region derives mostly from work in the woods. Loggers and logging have afforded countless incidents and tales based on them, some funny and some tragic, or a combination of each, but always ending with the unexpected.

It seems appropriate, then, that "tree art" is so conspicuous in this exhibition on the art of the Adirondacks. Rustic furniture was a sideline activity, more a hobby than an occupation, in which a small number of resident carpenters found an aptitude for close, imaginative labor. The entire tree—root, trunk, branch, twig, and bark—was utilized.

The Adirondack guideboat, which evolved in response to the region's network of lakes and streams, is the only other family of artifacts that might better embody the character of the Adirondacks. Story-telling and song are legitimate candidates not included (for reasons of presentation) but clearly belonging to a noteworthy native tradition perhaps more vital today than boat and furniture construction. The rigor of life in the Adirondacks allowed the women and girls little free time for domestic handiwork such as quilts and needlework. That, at least, is an explanation why so few such things have turned up since the Adirondack Museum opened in 1957.

There were other artistic expressions in the Adirondacks, to be sure, but these were reportage, usually by individuals who visited the Adirondacks and reported their findings to audiences somewhere else. Oil paintings and watercolors by artists such as Thomas Cole and Winslow Homer are examples. Lithographs, especially those executed by the firm of Currier & Ives after paintings by Arthur Fitzwilliam Tait, convinced middle-class Americans that outdoor scenes like those showing sportsmen and guides lolling contentedly in camp or on a pristine lake were worth attaining.

Photographs replaced lithographs and other forms of printmaking as the principal vehicle of graphic information about the Adirondacks. Seneca Ray Stoddard remains the most prolific and versatile of hundreds of serious photographers who came after him. His photographic career spanned a period that began in the early 1870s with the introduction of the railroad to the region and closed with the start of popular touring by automobile forty years later.

Considered adornments elsewhere, the arts of the Adirondacks have been the principal means by which the outside world has become acquainted with the region and its people. Historically outnumbered and fated always to remain so, Adirondackers may be forgiven for finding the passing scene close at hand to be more absorbing than events and people elsewhere. The material of their stories, like guideboats and rustic furniture, is locally grown. They trust the Adirondacks and feel a measure of pride for having made a nest here. This connectedness perhaps explains why many people, their ties to places and land elsewhere grown tenuous, have been returning to the Adirondacks for more than 150 years. The ritual, already five decades old when the Adirondack Park was created in 1892, continues to our day because the region remains open and vital. The challenge is for those who care—inhabitants and friends alike—to cooperate to keep it that way.

The Adirondack Park as Theatre

ANTHONY N. B. GARVAN

On May 2nd, 1892, Governor Flower of New York signed legislation creating the Adirondack Park, which was soon extended and confirmed by the courts. The passage of the Adirondack Park Enabling Act through a turbulent legislature overturned many predictions of defeat or blockage. An unlikely alliance of New York water officials, game hunters, physicians, conservationists, politicians, and the popular press easily overcame a weakened timber industry threatened by a further drought season of catastrophic forest fires.

Often cited as a surprising coincidence of climate, catastrophe, and influence, the legislation may have aroused as much nostalgia for past reality as for pioneering conservation. In fact, the Adirondack plateau of two to five thousand foot peaks had, at least in its historic past (beginning in 1688 when the Duke of York's proprietary became a Royal colony), much of the character of a park preserved from permanent European settlement by uncertainty of title, imprecise cartography, and severity of climate. At the same time, the area was open to hunters, trappers, and sportsmen willing to risk these hazards for pelts and the profitable Indian trade. Champlain's map of 1632 drew Indian villages east of Lake Ontario as smaller and less elaborate than those of western New York and, in his commentary as excerpted by E. B. Callaghan, as belonging to the Hurons. Settlement was in large part delayed until the Totten-Crossfield purchase and the nearly coincident death of William Johnson in 1777. Significantly, he left to his six Indian children claims of more than 15,000 acres of land along the east branch of the Canada Creek, which were surveyed and disputed as late as 1797.

The purchase from the Iroquois had opened the possibility of settlement on the plateau between Lake Ontario and Lake Champlain. War with Great Britain interrupted the survey and purchase of Totten-Crossfield. Only in 1792 did new surveys open the region to mining and timbering and bring to a close the beaver trade and scattered Indian title.

In the near century that lay between the MacComb survey and the drawing of the Blue Line, timbering and to a lesser extent mining dominated the Adirondacks. Water access by way of streams and dams permitted vast slash cuttings and extensive mill operations, connected, after 1850, by rail to all of the Northeast.

At the same time, in those parts of the Adirondacks inadequately served by fast streams and spring freshets like Township 40, time stood still. As late as 1855, Amelia Murray, Lady in Waiting to Queen Victoria, found the shores of Raquette Lake virtually unsettled and made her way to Old Forge without the benefit of stagecoach. As a result, climate and poor transportation preserved the material culture and the customs, indeed the personalities, of the hunters' frontier. Within three hundred miles of New York, more than a thousand miles east of Chicago, while the Gold Rush was settling California and the trans-Mississippi frontier was being settled along western railroads, Ned Buntline was writing from a shack at Blue Mountain and William H. H. Murray was recalling, in a strange mixture of fiction and instruction, his happy days at Raquette and Long Lake.

Anthony N. B. Garvan is Professor Emeritus of American Civilization at the University of Pennsylvania, Philadelphia, Pennsylvania. He is an author, raconteur, and native Adirondacker, having been born at Kamp Kill Kare. His sister, Marcia Anne Garvan Coyle, was his co-author in planning this article.

Although Samuel Howitt never witnessed American hunting, he relied on the detailed descriptions and sketches of English travelers and military officers for his *Foreign Field Sports*, published in 1814. Here he caught the main element of Anglo-American hunting of the black bear: the use of hounds shortened the drive and many shooters reduced the risk. The season is perhaps a trifle early as the trees still have some leaves and no snow is indicated. The late September 1813 date of this illustration is accurate for the fringes of the Adirondacks. "It is customary for a party of a dozen or twenty settlers to proceed out Bear-hunting. After many days residence in the woods, they return with a number of skins but the Indians are the most successful hunters as they have learned the value of the fur trade." Although Howitt mentions the occasional use of spears, his engraving shows only firearms and in every way is a functional, updated (1813) view of an American blend of French, British, and German hunting practices. Photograph from the author's collection.

Less than fifty years later, A. F. Tait's painting *A Tight Fix* (1858) illustrated the changes which had taken place. Two hunters have replaced the large party; tracking has replaced the drive, sport the fur trade. Perhaps also amateur ineptitude has replaced professional practice. The stance of the shooter and the knife of the fallen hunter do not suggest a happy outcome. Courtesy of the Manoogian Collection.

In *A Good Time Coming* (1867), A. F. Tait painted his most popular subject. His friend John S. Force, who has just arrived in his traveling clothes, pours himself a drink of champagne. Shooting companions have set out coffee, flour for pancakes, and are frying six small trout. Another of the party returns to the makeshift lean-to with a good catch and firearm. Two "deer dogs" about the size of harriers patiently await their share; nearby large-bore guns are stacked; at the landing a bent-wood canoe with a birch bark hull is beached, an anachronistic artifact suggesting the days of Indian occupation before 1774. The whole scene, even the temporary lean-to, reinforces the concept of an urban vacationer enjoying all the pleasures of wilderness sport, companionship, and isolation near the end of summer and only forty-five miles by coach from the Glens Falls railroad station. This painted image was given wide circulation by Currier and Ives and became the most complete visual image of the Adirondacks available throughout the state. Courtesy of The Adirondack Museum.

That literary image, combined with steamboat travel to Albany and railroad travel as far as Utica and Glens Falls, created frontier vacations first for the urban hunter, sportsman, and fisherman and later for his family. Perhaps even more influential than the literary texts were the colored lithographs by Currier and Ives and the straightforward wood-block engravings of the popular press. There one found the canoe, guideboat, rifle, deer dog, fly rod, backpack, lean-to, and snowshoe. Generally, these were used by male campers whose dress partially derived after 1865 from Civil War uniforms and conveyed the same camaraderie as Civil War camp scenes.

By narrow social and technological coincidences, parts of the Adirondacks had become theater in 1870. On its stage one play was enjoyed each summer and autumn. Called the American Frontier, it featured wild game, isolated huntsmen, and a forest apparently forever wild. Danger to life and limb was moderate until winter came in mid-December. Survival then depended upon the Adirondack guides' judgment and year-long residency. The hounds, snowshoes, and rifles became real artifacts of survival. The risks of weather, game, and exposure suitably exaggerated in popular prints became a wintry complement to the hunting expeditions of spring and autumn. The log lean-to in winter was not sufficient shelter, and one suspects the hunting parties included few visitors. The deer dog was now required to select a stag or doe and then to drive it for an initial shot. If that failed, pursuit on snowshoes would follow the cry of the deerhound without the added advantage of guideboat, flat-bottom, or canoe. Hounds were seldom aggressive or numerous enough to bring the deer to bay or to kill them without a rifle shot. As early as 1814, Howitt had described and drawn such a hunt of bear in Canada or northern New York where a party of a "dozen or twenty settlers" would hunt down several black bear over an extended hunt of several days.

Twelve years later (1874), Winslow Homer drew somewhat the same scene for a wood engraving in *Harper's Weekly* for November. A single hound rummages around the camp's perimeter while two companions doze and select fishing hooks near a small fire. A fair catch lies nearby, perhaps to be roasted in the coals. An extremely fragile lean-to supports a rod and perhaps a gun barrel. The absence of coffee, flour, pack basket, and luxuries suggests Adirondack year-long residents. Only the birch-bark covered canoe suggests the elaborate frontier ritual found in the paintings of Tait and others. Courtesy of The Adirondack Museum.

This tradition of plentiful game and high fur prices had died in the Adirondacks by 1840. Herbert Forester dates the deep snows of 1836 as the date of a final huge slaughter. By that time, white-tailed deer were scarce, beaver nearly unknown, wolves, elk, and moose almost extinct and bear uncommon. Small game, i.e. hare, rabbits, and foxes, supplied a modest but unglamorous game bag. Game birds, although stocked in New Hampshire, seem to have been available but not as plentiful as in the open farm lands south and west of the Adirondacks.

All these conditions were changed by the progress of lumbering. Despite losses to fire and flood, the new timbered lands provided vast new sources of berries and young forest growth that immensely benefited the white-tailed or Virginia deer, so that they had become by 1880 the prime target of hunters. These deer were portrayed in the paintings of the Adirondacks by A. F. Tait.

Tait's paintings were primarily for the printmaker, not the connoisseur. They were reproduced by Currier and Ives in a variety of sizes. Tait combined in these paintings landscape (Raquette and nearby lakes), Landseer-derived poses of stags and doe, and groups of game birds and deer arranged in scenes of domestic bliss. These recalled Victorian family portraits both European and American. Most popular were his images of hunting parties. In this way a highly popular image of wilderness or frontier life merged Civil War military male frugality with plentiful animal life—all arranged to mirror peaceful domestic human life far from industry.

Above all, this forest remained "Forever Wild," protected by the Adirondack Park Enabling Act of 1892 and then in 1894 by the New York State Constitution's Article Seven. In reality, the legislature, the administration, and the voters of New York State all knew that less than ten percent of the Forest Preserve and perhaps less than twenty percent of the privately held lands remained uncut in 1892. Almost everywhere, the white pines had been taken and perhaps fifty percent of the total park area, state, and private lands combined had been clear cut.

Under these circumstances, "Forever Wild" meant not preservation of an historic or prehistoric forest, but the reservation of existing land as the beginning of a vast land tract of millions of acres free from permanent settlement, timbering, or mining. In short, this first century of the Park is only its start. Its founders hoped to arrest human or cultural change and permit, but not nurture, forest growth. On the other hand, because animal and fish life had to supply annual game quotas, it was energetically restocked and protected. Deer, beaver, and bear recovered, though at an uneven pace. Elk and moose were reintroduced without permanent success. Bass, trout, and salmon were supplied from state and private hatcheries. Bird populations remained modest and suffered severely after 1950 from DDT spraying. Despite such failures and inconsistencies, the positive results of less than one hundred years of management of the Adirondack Park have been outstanding. The forest has in large part recovered and begun the long road toward maturity. Although the balance of species is not what it was in the nineteenth century, it has gained a character of its own suited to its own environment. Fire and pollution continue as threats but have been at least moderated. Above all, the permanent human population has not grown at national rates. Indeed, a few villages have declined in year-long residents. In this sense, the Park has remained a wilderness, its human population growth sharply reduced by climate and limited urban access.

These points are obvious to visitor and resident alike. What is a trifle more obscure is the stage at which policy has stopped the clock. There is no endeavor to reestablish the forest as it might have been in 1690 or 1790; instead, it is left to regenerate on the inheritance of 1890. The needs of residents and visitors are accommodated as well as may be in a forest that has been heavily cut, its animal and plant dictionary altered by extinction and restocking, and its communications (with the exception of the Northway) in a large part based upon their development in 1910. In short, the frontier clock stopped after the trapper, miner, and logger but before the farmer and townsman.

I have felt that anachronism throughout my life, and it has held a strong attraction for me. Born at Kamp Kill Kare in October 1917 in a large log boathouse completed only a few weeks earlier, I enjoyed the experience of childhood summers on a mile-long lake, some six and a half miles from Raquette Lake, then a small village and railroad depot. Each summer, my family would climb aboard sleeping cars in New York's Grand Central Station, shortly after July 4th. Cooled only by portable blowers, the cars were usually very hot until after Albany. Near dawn, the track began to penetrate woodlands and near seven a.m. reached Thendara. At that point, a diesel engine was connected to the Raquette Lake cars and the twenty-five mile ride began a slow ascent, offering the added advantage of a passing panorama of unbroken forest. Upon arrival at Raquette Lake, the train was met by an assortment of two and three-seater Glens Falls wagons, for supplies, equipment, and trunks. If lucky, I could ride on the lightest two-seater pulled by a pair of roans named for my parents, Frank and Mabel, and whipped up by Tommy Simmons dressed in flannel shirt, dungarees, and red suspenders. Such "comeuppance" wit was not lost on my parents.

Wit was a part of the larger household, which included a large family, numerous guests, cooks, butler and housekeeping staffs, gardener, boatman, guides and horsemen. From this unpromising roster, at least twice a week two baseball teams were recruited and nine innings played on an improvised field, and eventually there were uniforms, trimmed with green for the "Horseflies" and with red for the "Punkies." My father was non-playing captain of the "Horseflies," my eldest brother Pat, the leader of my team, the "Punkies." Not only boys like myself and friends played, but elderly gardeners and grooms were also pressed into service and subjected to ribald comments from family, guests, and fellow workers. To balance this emphasis on baseball, trails led to distant lean-tos where family and guides picnicked and camped. Bass and trout fishing supplied the Friday lunch for family and guests.

As the family was Catholic, Sunday Mass presented a problem in logistics, which was solved by transporting a priest from Raquette Lake and holding Mass, first in the dining room, later in a Norman style chapel to which worshippers from Uncas and Sagamore came by carriage.

Even though sermons might be shortened by my father's impatience, the service within the chapel was orthodox in every particular. Significantly, the chapel was removed from the main buildings and built from nearby quarried stone.

There a patriotic myth was manifest. The log cabin was a constant reminder of the tradition of log construction as the pioneer American architecture. This outward landscape was the setting for my father's strong isolationism. Deeply anti-British in a colonial Irish sense, he wrote, published, and publicly voiced his views, which bound his generosity to the Yale Art Gallery and his collections of American arts and crafts.

For Kamp Kill Kare, the six and a half miles of dirt road and the climb of more than two hundred feet provided the boundaries of a stage and guarded the rituals of frontier, baronial dining, primitive worship, and nineteenth century baseball from ridicule and criticism. Beyond such camp boundaries no such artificial isolation existed, but there too existed much the same unselfconscious playing of late frontier roles: huntsmen, storekeepers, tavern keepers, guides were enacted— only the horsemen and farmers rapidly declined, displaced by automobiles and foresters.

Most successful were the shooting and fishing lodges and their competitors, the big hotels. Both combined shelter and board with guided fishing and shooting expeditions though in different degrees of comfort and artificiality. Both stressed the importance of the native guide whose word was law and whose skills were central to the preparation of meals, choice of fishing or shooting sites, boating, and other emergencies. He did all the work but he also gave all the orders.

This rigid time-lock of the Adirondack self-image has certainly preserved much forest life, but it has had a price. First and most obvious, the Adirondack Park has, in its growth (now approximately half the area of Switzerland), developed no single center. In reality, it is an assemblage of many natural parks, separated by incongruous developments. The failure to develop a conservation policy toward buildings acquired by the Forest Preserve and scheduled for destruction has eliminated the usual center of forest preserves, as in Europe at Fontainebleau, Windsor, or Chantilly. The Park has lost many centers of interest.

Finally, and importantly, the Township, the basis of settlement and land allotment until 1900, has been gerrymandered out of all relation to geography or survey. In so doing, another path to at least local understanding between resident and visitor has been aborted and deflected.

The paradox of the frontier image remains. Economic growth that may benefit the town or year-long resident threatens, however remotely, the ecology of the wilderness and takes away the frontier stage as surely as the Depression destroyed the Great Camps of the past. Improvement in the Adirondack economy, however, may threaten the ecology. At the same time, if the ecology is harmed, the visitor economy will suffer. But if the ecology is too sternly preserved, the Park will be free of visitors, its trails neglected, its fires left burning.

A second paradox pertains to the cost of "Forever Wild," a paradox of a different order entirely. "Forever Wild" has been very successful with the Forest Preserve lands, but for private holdings it carries an implicit threat of contested title, public access, and destruction of all buildings. In a larger sense, speculators, conservationists, and those seeking to protect extant buildings on state land have been denied access to moderate solutions that would at once conserve forests and buildings. For example, the Park has an almost infinite variety of corporations,

On Lake Sumner the permanent sturdy will-built lean-to of hotels and boarding houses was copied by Lieutenant-Governor Woodruff and placed in an idyllic location to catch the sunset and his lake in all its moods. Hunting and fishing gear is placed nearby and the floor is boughed deeply with spruce and balsam branches. A bridge nearby leads to Bachelor's Island and a cabin.

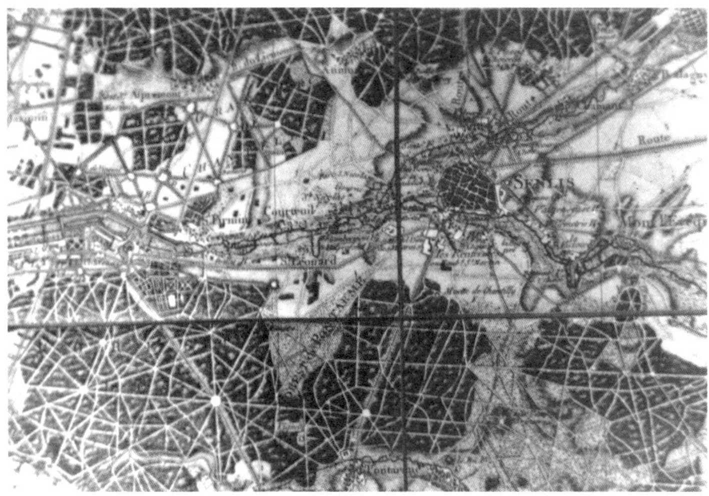

Senlis and the Forest of Chantilly near Paris, 1801. A typical French park designed for hunting and the timber industry is centered upon the chateau and town. Photograph from the author's collection.

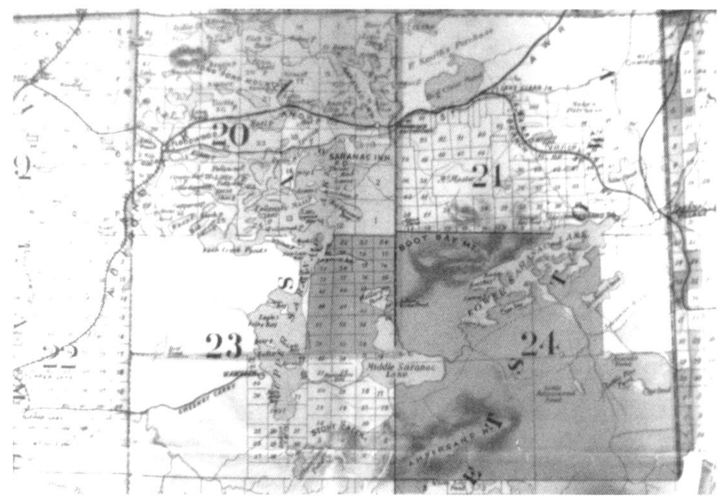

Adirondack Park, 1898. This detail shows Forest Preserve, private lands, railroad, and hamlet separated only by surveyed lines. No permanent roads, towns, or major buildings relate to the forest. Photograph from the author's collection.

partnerships, and charitable trusts within the Blue Line, but neither inside nor outside the Forest Preserve is there an Adirondack trust for historic preservation. Such a trust could be committed to the preservation of architectural, archaeological, and landscaped sites of primarily historic not natural importance. It would be supported by private and public funds and report directly to the Adirondack Park Agency.

By the same token, should not the question of selective forestry be solved on a rational basis by setting aside moderate acreages of clear-cut forest for selective planting before accepting them into the Forest Preserve? Sadly, the Uncas and Sagamore preserves, with the exception of the shoreline, were heavily timbered, following New York State policy and are now nearly impenetrable to canoeist, hunter, or hiker: a "Forever Wild" wilderness that requires an airplane to be viewed. Either would have been an ideal forest laboratory.

Finally, hamlets and townships are the chief demographic and political realities of the forest neighboring the Forest Preserve. Somehow, they must be included in the ongoing planning process for the Park; they cannot be treated as native reservations when they are custodians in fact, if not in law, of all the land within the Blue Line. They offer the best resource for the preservation of the Adirondack wilderness into the next century.

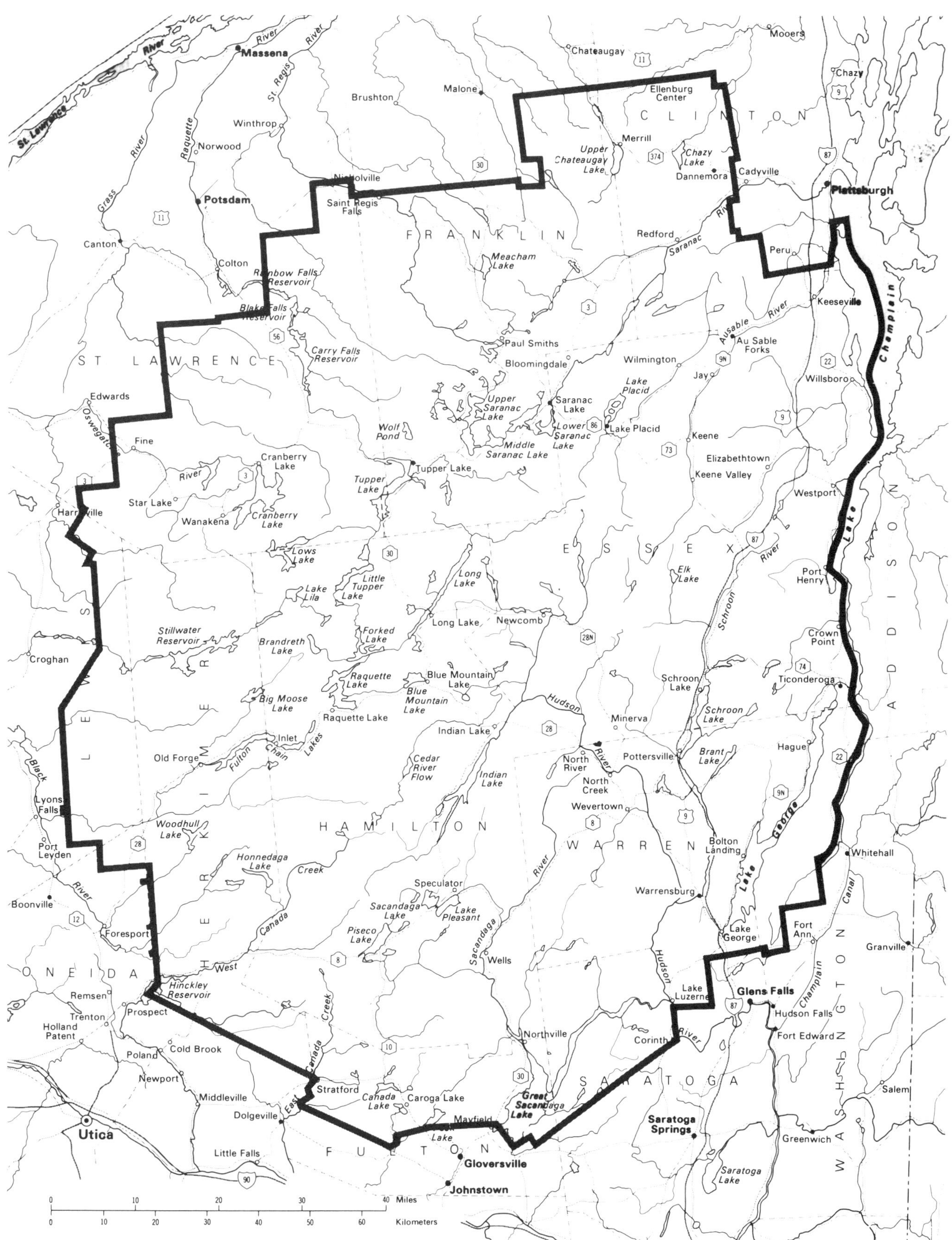

The Adirondack Park. Map courtesy of the Adirondack Park Agency.

The Space of Morality:
Death and Transfiguration in the Adirondacks

ROBERT L. McGRATH

No competing region of the country has served America's artists so well and for so long as the Adirondack north woods of New York State. In the protracted search for a distinctive cultural identity, its forests, lakes, and mountains have provided some of our best writers and painters with a potent landscape redolent of history, myth, and religion. Charged with a transfiguring freight of meaning, the Adirondack wilderness has been, from first to last, a space of morality.

Prior to the early Romantic period, less was known about the great north woods than about the Rocky Mountains or the Sierra Nevada. A blank area on the map, larger in size than the state of Massachusetts, the Adirondacks were a physical and cultural void awaiting exploration and exploitation, a place claimed on paper before it had been possessed.

When, during the early nineteenth century, the painter Thomas Cole visited the region around Schroon Mountain he described it as incarnating a "wild sort of beauty." In this he was referring to more than mere aesthetics. As a "higher landscape" the wilderness was for Cole a place for the encounter with the divine, in the painter's words: "yet a fitting place to speak of God."[1]

During that same summer of 1837, New York's highest mountain, Mount Marcy, was first climbed by a party of the State Natural History Survey, and a name was imparted to the region. The nearly simultaneous "invention" of the Adirondacks by artists and scientists during the early Romantic period constituted both its psychic geography and physical boundary.

The painter Cole's still earlier visit to Lake George, in the fall of 1826, was inspired by the recently published novel *The Last of the Mohicans* by his friend and admirer, James Fenimore Cooper. Transforming the historically charged ground that engendered Cooper's vision of the American hero in primordial space, Cole shaped a compelling image of death and renewal. (Fig. 1)

One of several extant canvases representing episodes from the novel, Cole's painting depicts the carnage described in the book's penultimate chapter.[2] In the dramatically lighted foreground, the murdered bodies of the incipient lovers Cora and Uncas lie at the feet of Hawk-eye who takes aim with his rifle at the evil Huron Magua. The latter, clinging to the face of an opposing rocky ledge, is balanced by Major Heywood who enters the deliberately theatrical setting at the left near a waterfall. In conformity with Cooper's and Cole's shared vision of American space, the figures are dwarfed by the vast sweep and immensity of nature. "Interminable forests" extend into the background where a storm rages, a natural adumbration of the emotional content of the painting. The real subject of the work, the Adirondack wilderness, eclipses human events, rendering them insignificant in the face of nature's grandeur. A stage too large to be mastered by human action, the great north woods is the major protagonist of Cole's pictorial drama.

At this early phase of his career, however, Cole felt that "simple nature," no matter how wild or vast, was insufficient to invest the landscape with higher

Robert L. McGrath is Professor of Art History at Dartmouth College, Hanover, New Hampshire. A popular lecturer, he is author of the catalogue and co-curator for the exhibition-in-preparation, *"A Wild Sort of Beauty:" Adirondack Art and Artists,* which will open in the summer of 1992 at The Adirondack Museum, Blue Mountain Lake, New York.

meaning. Rather, he sought through associations afforded by such literary works as *The Last of the Mohicans* to consecrate the land. As a locus of life and death, both for man and nature, the Adirondacks constitute the ground for regeneration through violence. A mythic region, defined less by maps than by myths, the north woods were at once the abode of evil and an earthly paradise.

About a decade later, Cole returned to the Adirondacks again seeking to elicit meaning from the great northern wilderness.[3] In the well-known painting entitled *Schroon Mountain* (Fig. 2) of 1838, the artist shapes a new vision of sublimely transcendent nature unencumbered by the associations of history and literature. A natural Eden, the unfallen world as originally created by God, the great north woods bodied forth Locke's dictum: "In the beginning all the world was America." Now superior to Europe, precisely because it was free from association ("no ruined tower to speak of outrage"), Cole's pictorial Adirondacks provided a brave new world for the American Adam. Enframed by writhing anthropomorphized trees, a forest of blazing autumn foliage prefigures the season of death. Above a limpid lake the pyramidal summit of a mountain penetrates the heavens. Encircled by halo-like clouds illumined by a shaft of radiant light, the peak beckons the devotee of nature to undertake a spiritual pilgrimage. In his diary Cole described his experience of the mountain: "We entered the wood and found it but a narrow strip. We emerged and our eyes were blessed . . . Below, stretched to the mountain's base a mighty mass of forest, unbroken but by the rising and sinking of the earth on which it stood. Here we felt the sublimity of untamed wilderness, and the majesty of the eternal mountains."[4]

Fig. 1. Thomas Cole, *Last of the Mohicans,* 1826. Oil on panel. Private Collection.

Fig. 2. Thomas Cole, *Schroon Mountain, Adirondacks.* Oil on canvas. The Cleveland Museum of Art, Hinman B. Hurlbut Collection.

Fig. 3. Homer Dodge Martin, *Lake Sanford, A Fire-Slash Lookout.* The Century Association, New York.

Recording his experience of the mountain as a sacred act, an ascent to "the everlasting throne," Cole envisioned his greatest numinous landscape. An image of natural Transfiguration, Cole's magisterial view is one of the greatest icons of nineteenth century American nature reverence. As a model for countless Hudson River School landscapes, *Schroon Mountain* projects an image of mountain glory signifying Romantic America's pantheistic devotion to nature.

A generation later, Homer Dodge Martin's *Lake Sanford, A Fire-Slash Lookout* (Fig. 3) provides a brooding counterpoise to Cole's transcendent mountain view. Constructed from a bird's eye vantage, Martin's canvas, with its morbid palette of browns and greys, stands in marked contrast to the brilliant autumnal colors of *Schroon Mountain.* From a stark rocky ledge, the spectator looks upon a burnt and eroded landscape that offers little ingress to a viewer searching for God-in-nature. Fire blasted spruces, standing like sentinels, direct the eye towards a decaying and melancholic world ravaged by fire and tempest. Receding light and tempestuous skies further intimate what has recently been described as the "twilight fears" of Tonalism.[5] In suffusing the view with an aura of gloom, Martin demythologizes the once resonant landscape. No longer a vehicle for historical or religious reflection, Martin's inner landscape reflects the private world of the painter's sensibility. As such, the wilderness can no longer bear the older freight of meaning. In *Lake Sanford* the Adirondacks expire in the throes of "Tonalist doubt."[6]

Winslow Homer's *Huntsman and Dogs* (Fig. 4) of 1891 imposes a still greater freight of violation upon the mental topography of the Adirondacks. Witnessing the continued cultural and physical erosion of the once consecrated ground, Homer's work alludes to the tragic myth of Diana and Actaeon. Against a ravaged mountainside, punctuated with scrubby second growth, a brutish "pot hunter" surges up against the landscape.[7] Leaping hounds who will soon turn on their master (already partially metamorphized into a deer), bay at their eventual prey.[8] The sacred groves of the goddess of conservation have been desecrated by lumbermen and venal hunters. Among Homer's many sources for this complex allegory of transgression are such Renaissance paintings as Titian's *Actaeon Attacked by Dogs*, which the artist surely knew from many visits to London's National Gallery.[9] Another probable influence, as well as a related use of the classical theme, is the cover illustration (Fig. 5) for *Harper's Weekly* for August 1883 where Miss Diana (an Adirondack Artemis and the embodiment of chaste American womanhood) stalks the wild deer.

Homer's remarkably complex reformulation of the myth of Diana and Actaeon doubtless reflects the artist's strong aversion to logging and hunting practices in the Adirondacks. In the year following this powerful work, and in response to similar outcries about the destruction of the forests, the New York State Legislature signed into law the bill creating the Adirondack State Park.[10]

Fig. 4. Winslow Homer, *Huntsman and Dogs*, 1891. Oil on canvas. Philadelphia Museum of Art: The William L. Elkins Collection.

Fig. 5. *Miss Diana in the Adirondacks— A Shot Across the Lake. Harper's Weekly,* August 25, 1883.

The symbolic stump reappears in the early modern period in the Canadian artist David Milne's *Painting Place No. 2* (Fig. 6). Executed in 1926 when the artist was in residence at Big Moose Lake in the Adirondacks, this striking view juxtaposes the blasted stump with the waters of a crystal lake and a distant range of mountains. The site of the murder immortalized in Theodore Dreiser's *American Tragedy* (published in 1925), Big Moose Lake is the body of water where, as Vincent Scully has provocatively observed, the American hero expires "at the place where he was born."[11] Milne's appropriation of this infamous place, both for its actual and literary resonance, is obviously more than coincidental. Significantly, Milne includes the accessories of his craft—paintbox with palette and brushes and a coffee jar, intimating that the cultural alliance, born with Cooper and Cole, is renewed in a modern collaboration of the sister arts.[12]

Tom Blackwell's *Hudson River Landscape* (Fig. 7) of 1985 provides a poignant closure to the series of Adirondack images. Reflecting upon the artistic past as well as the historical present, the painter underscores the now uneven dialectic between nature and culture. Blackwell's hyper-realist image contrasts a derelict car (Pontiac?) with the limpid river whose headwaters lie in the heart of the Adirondacks, and whose name denotes our greatest school of landscape painters. Eclipsing the natural vista, the wrecked automobile occupies the largest part of the field of vision and displaces the once sacred landscape with the detritus of a failed culture. The harsh dominance of man and his accessories over nature inverts the schematic relationship inaugurated by Cole over a century before. As a modern form of Apocalypse, Blackwell's image prophesies the end of nature. Closing the circle of death and Transfiguration, *Hudson River Landscape* charts the trajectory of America's painful and destructive passage from innocence to experience.

Fig. 6. David Milne, *Painting Place, Green No. 2.* Oil on canvas, mounted on Masonite. National Gallery of Canada, Ottawa. Gift from the Douglas M. Duncan Collection, 1970.

Fig. 7. Thomas Blackwell, *Hudson River Landscape, 1984.* Oil on canvas. The Currier Gallery of Art, Manchester, NH. Gift of Janet Hulings Bleicken, Robert P. Bass, Jr., Eleanor Briggs, Edith and Peter Milton, Charles and Mary Merrill and deKalb Fund.

NOTES

1. From Thomas Cole's *Essay on American Scenery* (1835) reprinted in John W. McCoubrey, *American Art 1900-1960, Sources and Documents* (Englewood Cliffs, New Jersey, 1965), p. 100.
2. The painting in the Katonah exhibition, *Indian Sacrifice*, has been variously described as *Landscape with Figures, The Death of Jane McCrea*, or, as is most likely, *Scene from Last of the Mohicans*. In his recently published study of the art of Thomas Cole, Ellwood Parry has argued persuasively for this latter identification. An oil sketch in the New-York Historical Society and a drawing in Detroit served as preparation for the finished work. Paintings in Hartford, Connecticut, and Cooperstown, New York, as well as the painting discussed above, make clear that Cole was obsessed with Cooper's novel at this stage of his career. See Ellwood C. Parry III, *The Art of Thomas Cole: Ambition and Imagination* (Newark, NJ, 1988), pp. 48 ff & figs. 25-27, 37, 40-41.
3. The account of Cole's later visits to the Adirondacks, taken from the artist's journals, is found in Louis Le Grand Noble, *The Life and Works of Thomas Cole* (ed. Elliot St. Vesell, Cambridge, Massachusetts, 1964), pp. 177 ff.
4. Ibid., p. 179.
5. See the provocative essay on Tonalism by Bram Dijkstra, "The High Cost of Parasols: Images of Women in Impressionist Art," in Patricia Trenton and William Gerdts, *California Light 1900-1930* (exhibition catalogue), Laguna Art Museum, Laguna Beach, California, 1990.
6. Ibid., p. 37.
7. Describing Homer's painting in 1892 Alfred Trumble wrote in *The Collector*: "Every tender mercy of nature seems to be frozen out of it, as if it were painted on a bitter cold day, in crystallized metallic colors on a chilled steel panel. He is just the sort of scoundrel, this fellow who hounds deer to death up in the Adirondacks for the couple of dollars the hide and horns bring in, and leaves the carcass to feed the carrion birds." Cited in Nicolai Cikovsky, Jr., *Winslow Homer* (New York, 1990), p. 111.
8. In the watercolor sketch for the composition (*Guide Carrying a Deer*, Portland, Maine Museum of Art), the young hunter carries a just-killed deer. In the final painting the dead animal has been reduced to a pelt and antlers draped over the guide like a second skin. See Helen A. Cooper, *Winslow Homer Watercolors* (New Haven, 1986), p. 176 and fig. 162.
9. Cf. Rodolfo Pallucchini, Tiziano (Florence, 1969), fig. 436.
10. Similar legislation against "hounding" deer with dogs was passed in 1885 only to be repealed two years later. Cf. Helen A. Cooper, op. cit., p. 194, n. 20.
11. Vincent Scully, *New World Visions of Household Gods and Sacred Places: American Art and the Metropolitan Museum of Art, 1650-1914* (New York, 1988), p. 115.
12. In the first version of the canvas (private collection), Milne included a writing pad in lieu of the paintbox indicating a shift from writing to painting. See Rosemarie Tovell, *David Milne, Painting Place* (Ottawa, 1976), figs. 5 and 6, pp. 11-12.

Adirondack Architecture and the Culture of Exurbia

PAUL MALO

In the mountains of northern New York, a distinctive regional architecture evolved during a half-century of building. Purporting to be rustic, indigenous, and artless, it is, in truth, cultivated, cosmopolitan, and artful. Adirondack architecture is not really vernacular: its characteristic style was forged with subtle rapport between native craftsmen and alien patrons, or in their stead, professional architects. Except for some local hotel entrepreneurs, the clients who commissioned major mountain buildings were not mountain folk,[1] and these remarkable buildings ought not be considered folk forms. Unlike the barn, which represented the reality of life and livelihood to the farmer, the mountain buildings considered here as architecture intentionally conveyed the unreality of a life that no longer depended upon livelihood.

The camp, the "Great Camp," as its larger species became known in the Adirondacks, was the most notable architectural form. Built as a second (or fourth or fifth) residence by wealthy urbanites, it was programmed for occasional, seasonal use, perhaps for only a few weeks of the year. The Adirondack camp, however, was different in kind from a contemporary cottage at Long Branch, or a castle at the Thousand Islands. The distinction was not merely one of architectural style, but of life style. Whereas one went to Newport in August primarily to drive in regal splendor up and down Bellevue Avenue, to see and be seen among the rich and famous, one went deep into the Adirondack woods to disappear from sight. One went to the Thousand Islands, another northern New York State resort not far from the Adirondacks, to consume conspicuously with steam yachts, basking in the admiration of steamboat excursionists for one's showplace island chateau, and to participate there in "the season" at grand hotels and yacht clubs. Conversely, in the Adirondacks one built a rustic hut on a thousand acres of wilderness. Even, as Tony Garvan of Kamp Kill Kare recalls, when one's nearest neighbors were Vanderbilts and Morgans, one did not go calling.[2] One only nodded reluctantly if by misfortune one should pass another on the road. The whole point of being in the woods was to escape.

Escape from what? What madness motivated families of ample means to stake camp in the damp, deep woods, with black flies for company? In what contemporary context did the primitive life of the savage appeal to those who could choose less arduous alternatives? In retrospect, we may suppose the call of the wild to be elemental. We may assume that all humans inevitably respond to unspoiled wilderness, evidencing innate human respect, even reverence, for nature. Balderdash. Seen in the longer perspective, this is a peculiarly modern sentiment. Our attitude towards the wilderness is a romantic, urban notion. In this light, Adirondack architecture may be understood as being profoundly anti-classical in spirit and, paradoxically, anti-rural.

The Rustic Hut, like the Noble Savage, is a modern invention, inherently a romantic, anti-classical and irrational fantasy. A Great Camp builder would have read *Robinson Crusoe* and *Swiss Family Robinson.* The notion of survival, of pre-

Paul Malo is Professor of Architecture at Syracuse University, Syracuse, New York. An author, he has written a book, *Landmarks of Rochester and Monroe County,* 1955, and numerous articles for periodicals. He is currently a member of the board of The Preservation League of New York State.

vailing in the wilderness, was central, as was the consequent requirement of self-sufficiency. One had to prove oneself in the hostile environment by one's wits and with one's own (or hired) hands. A Great Camp (like Marie Antoinette's Hameau at Versailles) would have had authentic cows, milked, to provide genuine cream. But do cows a farmer make? What real, common-sense farmer would ever stake a claim on such hard-scrabble, rocky hills?

There is something inherently preposterous in the notion of the Great Camp. Like mountain-climbing, as Tony Garvan recalls, it was done to prove that it could be done. The more improbable the proposition, the more satisfying the endeavor. If it seemed ridiculous at the outset for women, corseted and bustled, to be clambering over rocky slopes with parasols, the absurdity was heightened by their dining *al fresco* on linen with silver. The conceit continued throughout the era of the Great Camp. At Kamp Kill Kare, one invariably dressed for dinner, which might have been a veritable state function attended by the President of the United States and possibly a Cardinal, or a Bishop or two. Nonetheless, one was seated on backless benches to dine at a large indoor picnic table. Kill Kare was a camp, after all, even if spelled with a "K." Its complex of rustic buildings comprised a veritable museum, furnished with American antiques and especially commissioned works of decorative art.[3] One did not prove so much merely by surviving in the hostile wilderness; one proved more by prevailing there, in style.

Adirondack architecture warrants appreciation because it is significant; that is to say, because these architectural forms may be read as signs, as icons conveying meaning. To understand Adirondack architecture as it evolved between the 1870s and 1930s, one should recall the conditions of the times, the attitudes of the builders. Adirondack architecture speaks to us about life and nature, about one's place in a world becoming increasingly unnatural.

The Times

The Romantic view of nature may be discerned emerging in the later eighteenth century, concurrent with the disintegration of the *ancien regime* and the classical world view it espoused. Our new nation was not merely identified with the New World, but with a new world view. It was not until popular American culture began to emerge, identified with the presidency of Jackson and the spirit of the West, however, that the hegemony of an Eastern aristocratic tradition was supplanted, as silk knee breeches were given up in favor of populist trousers.[4] This cultural revolution was Romantic, in opposition to traditional Classicism. Nature was superior to inherited civilization. Unlike the old high culture, which had been restricted to connoisseurs, nature now was accessible, freely available to all. One required no formal education to be awed by storms, waterfalls, or formidable mountains. Nature spoke directly, intimately, to the common man.

> "To him who in the love of Nature holds
> Communion with her visible forms, she speaks
> . . .
> Into his darker musings, with a mild
> And healing sympathy that steals away
> Their sharpness ere he is aware.
> . . .
> Go forth, under the open sky, and list
> To Nature's teachings, while from all around-
> Earth and her waters, and the depths of air-
> Comes a still voice-" . . .[5]

But aristocratic William Cullen Bryant was premature. Nature did not yet speak to all, and he did not yet speak for the common man in pre-Civil War America. On the contrary, "they are insensible to the wonders of inanimate nature and they may be said not to perceive the mighty forests that surround them until they fall beneath the hatchet."[6]

It was not until Americans migrated from country to city in increasing numbers that they yearned for some "still voice" of Nature. Cultural orientation of the late nineteenth century, when Adirondack architecture began to take form, was confused, often inherently self-contradictory (a condition which seems to have continued to our own time). A growing urban elite cultivated an elaborate social protocol, while at the same time other Americans maintained that "virile men were rough men," and "good manners suspect."[7] While Americans avowed commonly shared democratic ideals, populist agitation increased among some of them, concurrent with escalation of aristocratic ambitions among others. Americans confronted dilemmas everywhere, as new values contested old, trying sentiments and loyalties. The Civil War had been the great unforgettable central crisis of the century for Americans, a familial confrontation and tragic conflict, a dialectical rite of change. Its impact was profound and lasting.

Adirondack architecture is a post-Civil War phenomenon. The first significant development began in the ensuing decade, as Americans began to retreat to the woods. Why? In reaction to the terrible collective action required by war, Americans turned from the older republican tradition of civic virtue, rejecting communal responsibility. They became egoistic, or at least devoted almost exclusively to family and kin. They became selfish.

The collapse of public morality was a self-fulfilling prophecy: some of the self-serving rushed in to fill the vacuum. As government became increasingly corrupt, fewer decent citizens would serve. The political boss of New York was convicted as a criminal; even the President of the United States was contaminated by the greed of his associates. The malaise was grave. In the 1870s, just as the Great Camp movement began, *The Gilded Age* was a Broadway hit. The term, coined by Mark Twain and Charles Dudley Warner as the title of their recent novel, became the characterization of an era. The gilt, quickly tarnished, was a cheap cosmetic vainly applied to hide, as Walt Whitman put it, "a deep disease, ... a hollowness at heart."

Many saw the city, the modern metropolis, as culprit. The older, agrarian virtues had been lost by new urbanites. The city was but symptom, of course. The Industrial Revolution had caused the modern metropolis. Ironically, those who had participated most effectively in the industrialization of America were precisely those now able to flee the modern world of their invention, to retreat back into the woods. Adirondack architecture as we know it, rustic though it pretends to be, is a product of modern industrialization. It required the patronage of urban wealth. These landmark works of rustic art are, oddly, but in very large part, memorials to American railroads and their builders.

The Railroads
Improved modes of transportation enabled growth of the metropolis. Canals built during the early nineteenth century, then railroads at the mid-century, expanded distribution of goods, produced by increasingly specialized labor concentrated in growing cities. Railroads provided both materials for urban production and commodities for urban consumption. The railroads were the first truly modern industry, requiring assemblage of vast capital, entailing participation of multiple investors. The first great corporations enabled the first truly national industry.

The first Adirondack Great Camp was created with new railroad wealth, derived from the pioneer transcontinental line. A famous golden spike linked America's two seacoasts by rail. Dr. Thomas Clark Durant drove that spike. It connected Durant's Union Pacific Railroad with the Central Pacific of Collis P. Huntington. The Durants built the first Great Camp, Pine Knot. Huntington later purchased it. Subsequently, the Kildare Club was frequented by railroad men, some of whom,

Vanderbilts, Webbs, and others, expended railroad wealth on Great Camps of their own. Other Adirondack campers, like the Brady-Garvans, were interested in urban transportation—elevated trains, street trolleys, and subways—as well as other utilities.

Promoters of railroads, particularly those lines that opened new territory for development, realized great profit from the sale of nearby land. Railroad builders became land speculators and lordly land owners. William Seward Webb acquired more than 225 square miles of the Adirondacks, his domain, Ne-Ha-Sa-Ne, being the largest of many vast mountain estates. Webb built a railroad through the mountains, giving access not only to his own Great Camp, but to much of the region.[8]

Earlier, the transcontinental railroad builder, Dr. Thomas Clark Durant, had constructed another road, insignificant nationally, but important to opening the Adirondacks. It had extended only from Saratoga Springs to North Creek, but gave entry into the vast region, where Dr. Durant had invested heavily in land. Foreseeing its development potential, in 1874 he recalled his son, William West Durant, from abroad to undertake building a Durant mountain empire.

The Great Camps of William West Durant
The younger Durant played a central role in Adirondack history and in the formulation of Adirondack architecture. Something of a Poor Little Rich Boy, his poignant life story has been well told by others.[9] If his plans for an Adirondack empire failed, he was more successful as an artist than as a business man. The Great Camp, as a work of art and a way of life, owes much to William West Durant.

Young Durant came to the Central Adirondacks in the 1870s, pitching tents at Raquette Lake, then contriving, from materials at hand, rustic cabins.[10] Eventually, his Camp Pine Knot became the first Great Camp and one of the finest, growing to become a veritable village of buildings, an experimental laboratory of rustic building techniques. Durant went on to build more ambitious camps: Sagamore, acquired by Alfred G. Vanderbilt, and Uncas, by J. P. Morgan.[11] He sold a smaller camp to Lt. Governor Timothy Woodruff of New York State, who improved it to become the nucleus of the Garvans' Kamp Kill Kare. These four Great Camps, all in the Raquette Lake area of the Central Adirondacks, comprise most of the extant Durant architectural legacy.[12]

Architecture was newly recognized as a profession in America when William West Durant began to indulge his passion for building. Untrained architecturally, he was a dilettante designer in the tradition of gentlemen who improved their estates. He showed little of his father's acumen, but evidenced taste, a good eye, and demanding standards of craftsmanship. Although Durant occasionally was assisted by practicing architects, the vision of the ideal Great Camp was his own.

Precedents for Adirondack Architecture
William West Durant, as son of a wealthy businessman, was exceptionally advantaged culturally. He had studied in England and on the Continent and undoubtedly was familiar with vernacular Alpine buildings. The Swiss chalet was a primary model for the Durant camps.[13]

The Swiss commonly folded the roof across the shorter dimension of the building rather than the longer, as is our prevailing practice. As a result, a very large, imposing gable extended across the broader facade. Again, contrary to a popular notion here that roofs in northern climes should be steep in order to shed snow, the Swiss favored lower pitches, the better to retain a deep blanket for winter insulation. These Swiss roofs overhang the walls on all sides broadly, sheltering doors, windows, porches, and balconies. Such arrangements produce the characteristic chalet form apparent at Camp Pine Knot's main building, even in its

earliest single-story version.[14] (Fig. 1) The Swiss weighted their roofs with rocks so that winds, catching the eaves, would not lift them. Durant held down roofing of peeled bark with logs.

When expanded by addition of a second story, the main building at Camp Pine Knot appeared to be even more Swiss. (Fig. 2) A second-story gallery, running around the entire building under its broad eaves, contributed to this effect. The tidy Swiss, however, would not have favored such rustic materials. They squared their logs rather than using them in the round with bark intact. Clearly in contrast, rusticity was Durant's aesthetic intention at Camp Pine Knot. Natural finishes prevailed, although Durant, ever concerned with practical detail, painted the vulnerable sawn log ends with red paint to avert moisture penetration; he used the same paint on milled wood for window sash, enlivening the somber character of the natural wood.

Even in the original version of Pine Knot's main building, Durant did not employ logs for the walls above window height, within the pediment formed by the roof gable, but introduced again the same peeled bark used on the roof, applied here like external wall paper. Surprisingly durable, tree bark became one of the most characteristic materials of the Adirondack style. When lifting the roof, Durant clad the entire second story of Camp Pine Knot's main building in cedar bark.

Although cedar bark was most commonly employed as exterior cladding, spruce and birch were occasionally used—the latter particularly for decorative panels—highlighted by the white color. Pliable twigs and saplings often were applied in decorative designs atop the birch bark—no doubt by the same local craftsmen who produced the fine rustic furnishings for the Durant camps.

The main building at Camp Pine Knot also shows an early instance, perhaps the first, of what was to become the veritable hallmark of Adirondack architecture: the decorative, truss-like linear arrangement of logs inserted within the pediment of the roof gable. This device has been employed consistently in the Adirondacks for more than a century.

In form, rustic character, color, and detail, the main building at Camp Pine Knot appears to be the progenitor of the Great Camp and a model for Adirondack architecture. Durant achieved here a synthesis of Swiss precedent and indigenous practice. Another formal model clearly was the local lumber camp, a collection of rustic shacks improvised from materials at hand. The buildings at Camp Pine Knot were not large, but they were many, with different structures serving different functions. The hazard of fire was real, and detachment was a precaution. Because the kitchen was especially vulnerable, it was detached, sometimes together with a dining hall. The promenade to dinner, through rain or dripping hemlocks, became a mountain ritual.

To facilitate circulation between detached buildings, Durant introduced at Pine Knot a covered wooden boardwalk raised about the wet ground. This roofed, but open-air, corridor became another familiar feature of Adirondack architecture, sometimes illuminated in the evening by kerosene lamps, or by Japanese paper lanterns.

The Japanese influence was also incorporated by Durant in his work. The Adirondack Great Camp emerged in the 1870s, when the influence of Japan, newly opened to the West, was apparent in all the decorative arts as well as in architecture.[15] A Japanese pavilion at the Philadelphia Centennial Exhibition of 1876 was widely admired, and novel features of Japanese architecture, like the fretwork seen within Japanese houses, were reproduced as the sort of decorative spindle panels so familiarly seen in archways of late nineteenth century American interiors. Similarly, lathe-turned woodwork (becoming known as "gingerbread") adorned exteriors as well, especially porches and within roof gables. Durant shared this period taste, but gave it rustic expression.

Even more Japanese, surely, was Durant's empathy with nature and his sensitivity about living intimately in the natural environment. Arranging a house as linked pavilions, circulating out-of-doors among the ferns, was very Japanese. Artful use of unfinished natural materials likewise recalls Japanese practice, particularly in tea-house design.

Beyond romantic, exotic tastes for the Alpine and Japanese, and in addition to local vernacular precedent, a more general American characteristic of the times was a component of Adirondack architecture. The Centennial of 1876 increased America's consciousness of its past. The Philadelphia exhibition revealed dramatically how, as America was coming of age, it was becoming industrialized, urban, and modern. "Early American" houses soon began to be built.[16] A great wave of nostalgia, fondly recalling lost youth and innocence, swept the land. The back-to-the-woods movement was seen not only in the Adirondacks, but at resorts everywhere.

Appreciation for nature was enhanced in the 1870s by new awareness that wilderness was a disappearing resource. "Go west," the young man had been advised, not long ago.[17] But now "all the good public lands fit for settlement are sold."[18] Disappearance of the American frontier would be confirmed by the Director of the 1890 census, but even in the '70s, at the time of the nation's first centennial, Americans were becoming aware that the era of the pioneer was at an end. In that decade "rough camping trips" became popular as antidote to the self-imposed decorum of a newly emerging, socially insecure urban society. The bicycle craze provided a wholesome urban outlet. Active participation in sports peaked in the '90s, when women became relatively liberated, at least sufficiently to engage in outdoor activities: croquet, lawn tennis, archery, canoeing, fishing, swimming—even shooting in the Adirondacks.

In the '80s there were practically no suburbs. One lived either in a town or in the country. Train travel was inconvenient and arduous. Urbanites might flee the city for a lengthy stay in the country, but only infrequently, and usually only for an annual summer vacation. It is difficult for us, given our mobility, to appreciate the yearning of families, trapped in a great metropolis, for the distant countryside, for remote, unspoiled wilderness.

"At no time in history have the human nerves suffered as they do now from the wild speed at which life travels, and the pressure of occupations and amusements. Leisure seems to be a thing of the past.... The philosophic speculator may perhaps see in the prevailing restlessness that of a generation who, having drifted away from the traditions of its forefathers, has not yet formulated the code that is to rule its future."[19]

Post-Civil War Americans fluctuated between mental bravado and moral despair. Americans could be boastful of growing prowess, yet critical about their powerlessness to cope with rapid change. On the one hand, they were collectively confident about prevailing as a nation, but on the other they withdrew personally into a mode of uncertain self-interest. There was, as Theodore Roosevelt observed, "almost no teaching of the need for collective action." The first wave of civic reform did not occur until after the turn of the century, when Roosevelt and others demonstrated renewed responsibility as leaders. Strenuous Teddy loved the out-of-doors and visited woodland havens such as Camp Santanoni in the Adirondacks, but was far too engaged in day-to-day combat to disappear for long into the backwoods.

Fig. 3. Santanoni as it appeared shortly after construction in the 1890s. The kitchen wing is at the left and guest cottages at the right. Photograph is from the Pruyn family albums, lent by Mrs. Thomas King II, Saratoga.

Self-reliance was integral to the Great Camp mystique. Emerson had identified this American trait.[20] The return to self-sufficiency, living off the land by one's own means, was a romantic motivation of Great Campers. They felled trees to build log houses and rustic furniture, even forged their own hardware on the site. They cut ice stored in ice houses, grew garden crops stored in root cellars, kept livestock, and churned butter. As camps became more grand, staff increased. Generations of Adirondackers were born, wed, and died on the vast mountain estates, visited only a few weeks of the year by their largely absentee owners.

Emerson's "Self Reliance" was integral to a cultural view shared by much of the educated American elite. Particularly identified with New England, this ideological current found another voice in Thoreau, who had retreated to a rustic hut at Walden Pond.[21] George Perkins Marsh became an early advocate of natural conservation and John Burroughs nature's eloquent spokesman.[22] A noted family of conservationists, the Marshalls were Adirondack Great Campers.[23] Taking care of one's own was not incompatible with taking care of the natural environment. Self-concern, so effectively ennobled by Herbert Spencer in late nineteenth century social doctrine as nature's way of improving the species, became compatible with concern for Nature, with the capital letter favored by the early nineteenth century Transcendentalists.

Other Great Camps
The Preservation League of New York State, concerned with saving landmark historical buildings of the Adirondacks, undertook a comprehensive survey of Adirondack Great Camps. Although incomplete, the study identified more than thirty major camps—too many to be discussed here.[24] Some of these, like Mabel Brady Garvan's Kamp Kill Kare and Marjorie Merriweather Post's Camp Topridge, are widely known, if not generally accessible to the public. William Rockefeller's Camp Wondundra has become a hostelry, enjoyed by small numbers of guests. Larger numbers visit the Vanderbilts' Camp Sagamore, now a conference center conducting regularly scheduled public tours. More remote of access, but belonging to the people of the State of New York, is one of the earliest and greatest of the Great Camps. It warrants particular mention here as a critical preservation problem.

Santanoni
A member of the older American aristocracy, Robert Clarence Pruyn built, in 1892, one of the major landmarks of the Adirondacks, Camp Santanoni.[25] Like William West Durant, young Robert Pruyn, son of distinguished parents, was culturally advantaged. He married Anna Martha Williams, daughter of an Albany banker. The Pruyn-Williams' family tastes for the arts, combined with fondness for the out-of-doors, no doubt inspired building Camp Santanoni. (Fig. 3) When Robert C. was forty-one, he and his wife, Anna, built a vast log villa on the estate to accommodate their family and its many distinguished camp guests, such as President Theodore Roosevelt. The Pruyns selected as their architect Robert Henderson Robertson, the New York City architect who became known as designer of the world's tallest building.[26] He also designed the main residence at Ne-Ha-Sa-Ne for William Seward Webb.

Shortly after being built, the log villa at Santanoni was described as "the largest and finest in the entire forest."[27] Its arrow-shaped plan linked many buildings by large covered decks, virtually outdoor rooms. Five buildings formed the arrow head, 265 feet in width. The main hall, situated at the tip, opened onto a lofty portico, which framed a vista of Santanoni Mountain across a large lake adorned with islands.[28]

In the gable of the portico, Robertson inserted the same sort of decorative log truss-work used by Durant at Camp Pine Knot. The color scheme is the same, red paint on milled window sash and doors contrasting with the natural brown of wood-shingle room and log walls.[29] Santanoni is the more striking, for here the logs have been peeled of bark and stained almost black with creosote.[30]

The main house at Santanoni is constructed of solid logs, more than fifteen hundred, cut on the estate. Over five thousand square feet of covered "piazzas" provide ample room for outdoor living, even in the frequently rainy mountain weather. Another prominent architectural firm, Delano and Aldrich, designed a stone-arched gate house and lodge and probably other stone estate buildings, such as a lake-side studio and the Creamery, a dairy building in the farm complex that is situated on the scenic entry drive, more than four miles long.

Santanoni was built "almost entirely by men from the neighboring Adirondack villages," realizing the vision of urbane owners and architect.[31] The log villa is a marvel of craftsmanship, but this is not naive, vernacular architecture. Like the work of Durant, whose influence is suggested here, Santanoni conveys a cosmopolitan character. Robert Pruyn's years spent in Japan seem to be recalled by the unique plan, so like an aristocratic Japanese villa, with pavilions extended by decks, arranged in stepping fashion to provide many external corners for outlook into the natural surroundings. The striking kitchen wing, forming the tail of the arrow, recalls Japanese log treasure houses, built to protect valuables from fire.[32]

Santanoni is less of an improvisation than Pine Knot. Most of the Durant camps "just grew;" Santanoni is more of a piece.[33] Robertson's great log villa is a powerful, unitary conception; its ancillary buildings, although equally fine, clearly were designed by another hand.

Santanoni, one of the most important works of Adirondack architecture, may be lost to the people of the State of New York, who own it. Little maintenance has been provided during two decades of State stewardship, since the buildings, according to one interpretation of Article Fourteen of the New York State Constitution, the "Forever Wild Clause," are illegal and ought to be demolished. The legal morass is too complex to discuss here, but a newly formed preservation organization, Adirondack Architectural Heritage, is leading a campaign to save this historic landmark of the region.[34]

Conclusion

Space does not allow a comprehensive survey of other Adirondack Great Camps, or adequate appreciation of important Adirondack architects such as William Coulter, Augustus Shepard, and their successors. Harvey Kaiser's large volume, as well as other books and articles, serve that purpose.[35] Rather, this essay has focused on the significance of Adirondack architecture, interpreting its meaning for those who made it.

During a half-century of change in America, some cultured urbanites who, like Henry Adams, were concerned that their way of life was becoming increasingly unnatural, sought to return to their roots, to live more closely with nature. Adirondack architecture, rather than being indigenously rustic, is really a culture of exurbia, a critical reaction to modern life. The Great Campers never became Noble Savages, of course. They did prevail in style—the Adirondack Style.

Between a place and its people, over a period of time, a mutual relationship develops. By a process of symbiosis, the place affects the people who live there, but at the same time, the people change the place, making it their own. The relationship between place and people is like a good marriage where, over the years, the partners become increasingly like one another.

The Adirondacks are a natural treasure, but our inheritance is more than a wilderness; it is a natural environment to which generations have attuned their lives. The makers of Adirondack architecture have bequeathed to us a way of life. Symbolized by the Great Camps, and lesser ones, Adirondack life has integrated the primeval and the urbane, as a model for living in harmony with the future.

NOTES

1. Some early hotels, like Henry van Hovenberg's built in 1880 at Lake Maria, were log structures. Others, like Ike Kenwell's contemporary structure, simulated log construction. Generally, the later, larger hotels favored a less rustic character, consistent with their more urbane life style.
2. Anthony N. B. Garvan, eloquent raconteur of Great Camp life, Professor Emeritus of American Civilization at the University of Pennsylvania, was born at Kamp Kill Kare in the Adirondacks.
3. The Garvans gave to Yale University the Garvan Collection of American Antiques, one of the finest in the nation.
4. Andrew Jackson was inaugurated as President in 1829. His predecessor, John Quincy Adams, was the first President to be seen officially in trousers. More aristocratic Federalists continued to wear breeches—Chief Justice Marshall until he died in 1835.
5. William Cullen Bryant (1794-1878), *Thanatopsis*, c. 1811.
6. Alexis De Tocqueville, c. 1831. *De la démocratie en Amérique*, 1835-40.
7. Henry F. Pringle, *Theodore Roosevelt* (New York, 1931), p. 47.
8. William Seward Webb, son-in-law of William H. Vanderbilt, had another estate at Shelburne, Vermont, where the Webb family maintains the Shelburne Museum. Webb's Adirondack and St. Lawrence Railroad, connecting Herkimer and Malone, was completed in 1892.
9. Craig Gilborn, Director of The Adirondack Museum, has written a major biography of William West Durant.
10. His father had some simple cabins already built on Long Point, which became the camp nucleus.
11. Sagamore and Uncas were both named for Native American characters in novels by James Fenimore Cooper. His *Last of the Mohicans* (1826) was particularly popular during the later nineteenth century, evidencing contemporary interest in the American past and life in a more natural world. Durant made other, nearby improvements to his properties, particularly an ambitious golf course development at Eagle Nest, but little building is extant there.
12. There are few architects of record for the Durant Camps. According to tradition, Durant designed the buildings himself, working closely with craftspeople. Extant at Uncas, however, an original drawing of some interior cabinetry indicates that Durant was assisted by others, at least in preparation of such drawings. Durant was continually experimenting, which may account for much of the variation in the character of his camps. Their style differs so greatly, however, as to suggest more contribution by several other designers than has been popularly recognized.
13. A Swiss music box, in the shape of a chalet, was literal model for another Durant building at Eagle's Nest.
14. Photographs show the building in the late '70s, without second story, and in the early '80s with raised roof.
15. Japanese influence in domestic architecture appears in period publications of the '70s, such as *Holley's Modern Dwellings*.
16. The Colonial Revival style evolved in the '80s, together with the related, more rustic Shingle Style.
17. "Go west, young men, go west" has been attributed to the New York City newspaper editor, Horace Greeley.
18. Major J. W. Powell, government geologist and "noted authority on the Far West," quoted by Samuel Reznck, in his *Business Depressions and Financial Panics* (New York, 1968).
19. Willet C. Cunnington, *Feminine Atttitudes in the Nineteenth Century* (New York, 1936).
20. Ralph Waldo Emerson's famous essay, "Self Reliance," was included in his *Essays, First Series,* published in 1841.
21. Henry David Thoreau's *Walden, or Life in the Woods* appeared in 1854.
22. George Perkins Marsh's *Man and Nature* appeared in 1864, his *The Earth as Modified by Human Action* in 1875 and 1885. The Hudson River naturalist, John Burroughs, an early supporter of Walt Whitman, published a series of works over a half century, beginning with *Wake Robin*, in 1871. John Muir's conservation-oriented writings were more recent, dating between 1916 and 1924.
23. Louis Marshall's family had a cottage at the Knollwood Club. Louis and his sons, Robert, George, and James, were leaders of the conservation movement in the Adirondacks and elsewhere.
24. Some additional properties have been identified since the survey was done; a few, such as Whitney Park, known to be one of the major private estates of the Adirondacks, were inaccessible.
25. Robert C. Pruyn's family was old Hudson River Dutch, descended from Franz Janse Pruyn, who came from Holland early in the 17th century to settle at Albany.
26. Robertson's Park Row Building, extant at 15 Park Row, between Ann and Beekman Streets in New York City, was the tallest building in the world when completed in 1899.
27. *Report of the Forest Commmmission*, New York State, 1893.
28. The name of the mountain which in turn gives the estate its name is supposedly a local Native American rendition of "St. Anthony" or "St. Antoine."
29. The trim color may not always have been red. A guest recalled it being white at one time. Photographs until the 1920s show the trim unpainted.
30. The bark was removed for the original construction, but the preservative was applied much later.
31. *Report of the Forest Commission*, New York State, 1893.
32. Young Robert was of an age to be aware of Japanese practice, serving as attaché to his father, the Ambassador.
33. Durant built Pine Knot over a longer period than Uncas and Sagamore; the latter two grew more during the tenure of subsequent owners.
34. Adirondack Architectural Heritage, Box 159, Raquette Lake, N.Y., 13436.
35. Harvey Kaiser, *Great Camps of the Adirondacks.*

The Future of the Adirondack Park

PAUL JAMIESON

In 1990 Neal Burdick, editor of *Adirondac*, invited several people he considered qualified to respond to the question: What will be the greatest difference between the Adirondacks of today and of the year 2000? Ten responses brought ten different viewpoints. The fact that they differed so widely on a mere decade of change is a lesson in humility for anyone forecasting the next one hundred years. The Commission on the Adirondacks in the Twenty-First Century has rendered its report. Its 245 recommendations have now entered the realm of politics and compromise, the final results of which no one can confidently predict. Even if all major recommendations should be adopted, forces beyond state control, such as acid rain and greenhouse effect, also impinge on the Park. In view of all these variables, one is forced to a subjective opinion: Within the realm of probability, what kind of park would I, based on my own experience and values, like to survive into the twenty-first century?

I am an outsider. My experience over the last sixty-two years has been that of going in, year round, for a day, for a camping trip of several days, or, accompanied by my wife, just for a drive through the Park and sojourn at a motor inn. My favorite recreations are observing nature, trail hiking, bushwhacking, snowshoeing, and canoeing. Once, when an attractively sited camp came on the market, I was strongly tempted to buy it. But on reflection I decided not to. To take one Adirondack camp off the market meant that eventually someone else would build another and thereby diminish the open space I prize. And I did not want to import into the woods the quotidian cares that attend a home owner on the outside. Above all, I did not want to become wedded to one corner of the woods. The Park is large enough to invite a lifetime of foot-and-paddle exploration.

I prize the Adirondacks as a refuge of peace, serenity, and adventure. In this I believe I have much in common with the seventy million who live within a day's drive. Even those who never go in derive satisfaction from knowing the Park exists, a remnant of our national heritage of wilderness. They want the Adirondacks to be as different as possible from the place where they earn a living.

There is a mystique about going in. It is symbolized on one entrance road by a large boulder known as Sunday Rock. For many generations the rock has been legendary as the division between two different worlds, the workaday, civilized one and the free, playful world of the great woods, where there are no obligations of a Sunday or any other day. Passing the rock, going in, is a ceremony of transition. We leave the world of linear time, which governs most of our lives in growing up, marrying, working for a living, raising children, growing old, and dying. In linear time there is no return. But in the woods we can experience a brief immersion in the cyclical time of nature and the cosmos, "a playful spin." William Chapman White beautifully expresses this immersion in his *Adirondack Country*: "As a man tramps the woods to the lake he knows he will find pines and lilies, blue heron and golden shiners, shadows on the rocks and the glint of light on the wavelets, just as they were in the summer of 1354, as they will be in 2054 and beyond. He

Paul Jamieson was Professor of English at St. Lawrence University, Canton, New York. An Adirondack Park intimate, he has explored its mountains, woods, and waterways throughout his adult life. Now retired, he is an avid canoeist and author. His books include *The Adirondack Reader*, 1964; *Adirondack Canoe Waters: North Flow*, 1975; and *Adirondack Pilgrimage*, 1986.

can stand on a rock by the shore and be in a past he could not have known, in a future he will never see. He can be part of time that was and time yet to come." As long as the Adirondacks offers this kind of experience, we can be hopeful about its future.

A poll sponsored by the Adirondack Museum in 1990 shows that a majority believes environmental conditions have deteriorated in the last ten years. Most of Neal Burdick's respondents are equally pessimistic about the next decade. The gift of silence will be further eroded, they say, cuteness will take over the road sides, additional second homes and condominiums will reduce the Park's grandeur, the Park will become another Vermont, political compromises in implementing the Commission's report will satisfy no one, and the Adirondacks will become increasingly a rich man's playground.

These are plausible views of the immediate past and future. Yet they seem to me one-sided in their pessimism. I cannot foresee a time when the kind of experience described by White will be impossible to come by. Safeguards are firmly in place in the forty-three percent of Forest Preserve land in the Park, protected under the "Forever-Wild" constitutional amendment of 1894, the strongest preservation law in the country. The enchantment of cyclical time may require more physical effort and ingenuity to attain than at present. It may not be available at all to those who simply drive through the Park. But it will be there in the recesses of the Forest Preserve, particularly in the million acres classified as wilderness, for those who seek it and know how to find it.

It is desirable, nevertheless, to make the enchantment available to the casual visitor. The two new Interpretive Centers recently opened are a step in this direction. The recommendations of the Adirondack Commission of 1990 would enlarge the Forest Preserve by some 650,000 acres of choice timberland and conserve open space in the private lands of the Park. Legislative approval of a substantial portion of the 245 proposals would go far to guarantee the preservation of the Adirondacks as the foremost wilderness area east of the Mississippi.

Preservation of open space is the key to the future. Risk factors differ among the four categories of space—travel corridors, settlements, back country, and waterways. Awaiting the motor tourist are hundreds of miles of roads bordered by dark conifers or by a mixed forest that awakens each spring in delicate pastel colors and subsides in fall in flaming brilliance. Driving through this wall of trees brings a sense of freshness and linkage to the natural world. Here and there the wall opens to modest views of mountain, lake, or river. The Commission report of 1970 listed forty scenic vistas. In the last twenty years, a few of these have already been lost to vegetation or development. One of the finest, the view of Whiteface Mountain across a broad expanse of Lake Placid, is now blocked by condominiums. Travel corridors are at high risk because most of the land they traverse is private and subject to development.

Back country is at risk because of the desire of second-home buyers for seclusion and for the very aesthetic features most threatened by increased development. Over seventy percent of all vacation homes in the Adirondacks are located on lakes, ponds, or rivers. The Commissions of both 1970 and 1990 address this issue by seeking to divert development toward the settlements and away from back country. It will not be easy to accomplish this. The isolated beauty of back country is a popular attraction for subdividers and summer residents. Yet every new subdivision, each new vacation home, diminishes the open space that is the Park's essential character. Adoption of the zoning provisions of the 1970 Commission's report has not prevented the creation of thousands of new building lots in the last twenty years. The 1990 Commission seeks a more drastic remedy in the transfer of development rights from back country to settlements. At this time, it is too early to predict success. The second-home buyer will not easily be persuaded that he can enjoy the Park without owning a choice piece of it.

I am more optimistic about the future of the waterways. Some twelve hundred miles of Adirondack rivers are zoned against harmful development under the State's Wild, Scenic and Recreational Rivers Act. And there is a good chance for passage of measures that restrict development on lake shores. But most promising for the future is the opening to public navigation of Adirondack rivers where right of passage has been denied for up to one hundred years.

Water is the most important recreational resource of the Adirondacks. The Park is unique in the lower states in combining mountainous terrain with an

Upper AuSable Lake from Boreas Bay.
Photograph by Seneca Ray Stoddard,
1887. Courtesy of The Adirondack
Museum.

intricate network of waterways. Besides 2,759 lakes and ponds greater than a half
acre in surface area, thirty river systems flow from interior elevations to the
perimeter of the dome-shaped uplift. Those main-stem rivers have numerous
tributaries, many of which are navigable and form cross-grained interconnections,
so that geography makes possible cruises of a hundred miles or more in all direc-
tions. All of this network was open to the public in the nineteenth century. The
Adirondacks was then the nation's favorite region for small-boat travel.

About 1890, however, the owners of large private parks, with the acquiescence
of the State, began to post river corridors and chain lakes against trespass. In the
present century, this practice was also followed by the game clubs that lease
corporate timberlands. Boating opportunities have been sharply curtailed for up
to one hundred years.

Now the situation is changing. A professor of law at Pace University, John A.
Humbach, in an exhaustive study of common and case law on navigation on inland
waters, concludes that there is a public easement on all rivers navigable in fact,
and that this easement is held in trust by the State. The Department of Environmental Conservation has adopted this study as a guide to future policy. It has
issued orders to field personnel to cease ticketing boaters for trespass on navigable
streams, and it is preparing regulations that name the navigable streams of the
state and affirm public right of passage on them. At the same time, awaiting action
by the legislature, is a rivers bill that will give the force of statutory law to right
of passage.

Valid reasons can be found to deplore the outlook for the Park in the increase
of the noise level, over-use of mountain trails, invasion of the back country by
summer residents, increased traffic and development in travel corridors, acidi-
fication of high-altitude lakes, etc., but, for this writer, recognition of the public's
right of passage on navigable rivers and streams opens a whole new realm of
recreational enjoyment. Wild river corridors are the museum galleries of the
natural world. The supreme kind of forest recreation is paddling a canoe in
tandem down a winding balsam-spired stream or across a lonesome pond bordered by piny eskers. This is the outlook for the twenty-first century, just as it
was a reality in the nineteenth, when W. H. H. Murray hailed the Adirondacks
as a paradise for boaters beyond all rivals, east or west.

Works in the Exhibition

Paintings, Drawings, and Prints

Anonymous
Blue Mountain
Oil on canvas
16½ × 29 inches
Eleanor B. Wunderlich

Anonymous
Adirondack Camping Scene
Oil on board
8½ × 12½ inches
John C. Wunderlich

Charles Baker
*A Recollection of the Adirondacks, Camp
Preston Pond*, 1854
Oil on wood
10 × 15 inches
John C. Wunderlich

Allen Blagden
September Snow—Loon, ca. 1986
Watercolor on paper
25 × 40 inches
The Adirondack Museum, Blue Mountain
Lake, New York

Ralph Blakelock
Untitled: The Log Cabin, ca. 1890
Oil on board
12 × 10 inches
The Adirondack Museum, Blue Mountain
Lake, New York

Allan Brooks
Spruce Grouse, 1921
Watercolor on paper
10 × 14 inches
Eleanor B. Wunderlich

Bufford's Lithograph (after Ebenezer
Emmons)
View of the Adirondack Mountains, 1838
Hand tinted lithograph
7½ × 12½ inches
The Adirondack Museum, Blue Mountain
Lake, New York

James E. Butterworth
Fort William Henry Hotel, Lake George,
ca. 1870
Oil on board
7 × 9 inches
The Adirondack Museum, Blue Mountain
Lake, New York

John Casilear
*Untitled: Keene Valley, Adirondacks, New
York*, 1881
Oil on canvas
14 × 20 inches
The Adirondack Museum, Blue Mountain
Lake, New York

Thomas Cole
Indian Sacrifice, 1827
Oil on canvas
36 × 48 inches
Van Pelt Library, University of
Pennsylvania

Samuel Colman
Untitled: AuSable River, ca. 1869
Oil on canvas
30 × 40 inches
The Adirondack Museum, Blue Mountain
Lake, New York

Verplanck Colvin
Lake Tear of the Clouds
Plate 1, Survey Book and Report of 1873
Colored lithograph
5¾ × 9½ inches
The Adirondack Museum, Blue Mountain
Lake, New York

Jasper Cropsey
Sunset, Lake George, 1867
Oil on canvas
24 × 44 inches
The New-York Historical Society

Currier & Ives (after A. F. Tait)
(Katonah only)
American Hunting Scene: An Early Start,
1863
Colored lithograph
24 × 31½ inches
Private Collection

Currier & Ives (after L. Maurer)
Camping Out: Some of the Right Sort, 1856
Colored lithograph
21 × 27 inches
Private Collection

Asher B. Durand
*Lake George View of Black Mountain from
the Harbor Island*, 1873
Oil on canvas
32½ × 60 inches
The New-York Historical Society

Asher B. Durand
*Adirondack Mountain Landscape,
Elizabethtown, N. Y.*, ca. 1848
Pencil on paper
10 × 14 inches
The New-York Historical Society

Louis W. Eilshemius
Near Giants' Mountain, 1883
Pencil on paper
14 × 11 inches
The Adirondack Museum, Blue Mountain
Lake, New York

Lewis Evans (Katonah only)
Map of Middle British Colonies, 1756
Publisher: James Turner, Philadelphia,
1775
18 × 24 inches
American Antiquarian Society, Worcester,
Massachusetts

Henry Ferguson
Glens Falls, 1892
Oil on canvas
15 × 26 inches
The Crandall Library, Glens Falls,
New York

A. B. Frost (Katonah only)
"We've Got Him Sure," 1882-83
Oil on canvas
15½ × 10½ inches
Private Collection

Hughson Hawley
Mountain Lodge, 1914
Watercolor on paper
24 × 45 inches
Adirondack League Club, Old Forge,
New York

Winslow Homer
A Good One, Adirondacks, 1889
Watercolor on paper
12 × 19½ inches
The Hyde Collection, Glens Falls,
New York

Winslow Homer
Fishing in the North Woods, 1896
Chromolithograph after Homer
15 × 21 inches
Sterling and Francine Clark Institute,
Williamstown, Massachusetts

Winslow Homer
Fly Fishing, Saranac Lake, 1889
Etching with aquatint on paper
14 × 22 inches
Sterling and Francine Clark Institute,
Williamstown, Massachusetts

Rockwell Kent
Asgaard Jerseys, 1965
Oil on canvas
35 × 44½ inches
Kent Collection, SUNY, Plattsburgh,
New York

Charles Lanman
Untitled: Temporary Camp, n. d.
Oil on canvas
18 × 24 inches
The Adirondack Museum, Blue Mountain
Lake, New York

Jonas Lie
Kamp Kill Kare, February, 1930
Oil on canvas
39 × 49 inches
Mr. and Mrs. Anthony N. B. Garvan

Homer Martin
In the Adirondacks (Saranac Lake), n. d.
Oil on canvas
12 × 19½ inches
Eleanor B. Wunderlich

Homer Martin
Adirondack Lake, 1869
Oil on canvas
8½ × 12½ inches
John C. Wunderlich

Jervis McEntee
Wood's Cabin on Rackett [sic] *Lake*, 1851
Pencil on paper
11 × 13 inches
The Adirondack Museum, Blue Mountain
Lake, New York

Levi Wells Prentice
Camping by the Shore, n. d.
Oil on canvas
12 × 18 inches
The Adirondack Museum, Blue Mountain
Lake, New York

Frederic Remington
Cabin in the Woods, ca. 1890
Oil on canvas
28½ × 20½ inches
Frederic Remington Art Museum,
Ogdensburg, New York

Frederic Remington
End of Day, 1904
Oil on canvas
27 × 40 inches
Frederic Remington Art Museum,
Ogdensburg, New York

Frederic Remington
Rushton American Travelling Canoe,
ca. 1886
Ink on paper
8 × 10 inches
The Benton Board, Canton Free Library,
Canton, New York

Frederic Remington
Rushton Toboggan, ca. 1886
Ink on paper
11 × 13 inches
The Benton Board, Canton Free Library,
Canton, New York

Frederic Remington
Running a Rapid, ca. 1890
Pencil on paper
12 × 9 inches
Frederic Remington Art Museum,
Ogdensburg, New York

Frederic Remington
Snaking Up a Rapid, ca. 1890
Pencil on paper
12 × 9 inches
Frederic Remington Art Museum,
Ogdensburg, New York

Frederic Remington
Towing Up a Rapid, ca. 1890
Watercolor on paper
11½ × 9 inches
Frederic Remington Art Museum,
Ogdensburg, New York

J. D. Smillie
Top of Giants' Leap, Adirondacks, 1869
Watercolor on paper
20 × 13 inches
The Adirondack Museum, Blue Mountain
Lake, New York

William J. Stillman
*The Philosophers' Camp in the
Adirondacks*, 1858
Oil on canvas
20 × 30 inches
Concord Free Library, Concord,
Massachusetts

Seneca Ray Stoddard
Along the Upper Hudson, ca. 1870
Oil on academy board
2¼ × 7½ inches
The Adirondack Museum, Blue Mountain
Lake, New York

Seneca Ray Stoddard
*In the Drowned Lands of the Raquette
River*, ca. 1888
Monochrome oil on academy board
6 × 8 inches
The Adirondack Museum, Blue Mountain
Lake, New York

Arthur F. Tait
A Natural Fisherman, 1875
Oil on canvas
14 × 22 inches
The Adirondack Museum, Blue Mountain
Lake, New York

Arthur F. Tait
Mink Trapping in Northern New York,
1862
Oil on canvas
20½ × 30½ inches
Munson-Williams-Proctor Institute
Museum of Art, Utica, New York

Eliphalet Terry
Untitled: Still Life with Creel and Trout, n.d.
Oil on canvas
17 × 22 inches
Private Collection

Worthington Whittredge
Sunlit Wood Scene, n. d.
Oil on canvas
15 × 16 inches
Eleanor B. Wunderlich

**Photographs from The Adirondack
Museum Collection**

G. W. Baldwin
Bicycle Club, ca. 1888
Silver print
8 × 9½ inches

*Loggers, Logs and Horses, Collecting Wood
for Winter*, ca. 1900
Silver print
6 × 8 inches

Horses Pulling Sledge with Logs in Snow,
ca. 1900
Silver print
4½ × 6½ inches

Loggers in Action on River, ca. 1900
Silver print
4½ × 6½ inches

Smelting Iron Ore, 1888
Silver print
4½ × 8 inches

David Marsh Camp, ca. 1888
Silver print
6¼ × 8¼ inches

Piseco Outlet (ladies fishing), ca. 1895
Silver print
4½ × 6½ inches

Edward Bierstadt
*Prospect House, Blue Mountain Lake, East
View*, ca. 1886
Silver print
5½ × 7½ inches

Duryea's Cottage, Blue Mountain Lake, ca.
1886
Silver print
5½ × 7½ inches

George Marshall

The First Forty-Sixers, ca. 1920
Silver print
8 × 10 inches

B. J. McCormick

Loggers with Peaveys by River, ca. 1900
Silver print
6¼ × 8¼ inches

Rev. Ormondo Putnam

Loggers with Double Bitted Axes, ca. 1885
Silver print
6½ × 8½ inches

Seneca Ray Stoddard

Pine Knot, ca. 1877
Silver print
4¼ × 7½ inches

Upper AuSable Lake from Boreas Bay, 1887
Original albumen print
14½ × 18½ inches

Sagamore, (three photographs), 1892
Original bromide prints
14½ × 48½ inches

Pine Knot (and ladies), 1888
Silver print
13½ × 17 inches

In the Adirondacks, Adirondacks, 1889
Silver print
14½ × 18½ inches

Blue Mountain Lake House, Adirondacks, 1889
Silver print
6½ × 8½ inches

Paddling Race 1885 "Viva," "Bijou", "Maggie", 1885
Silver print
4½ × 7½ inches

O. S. Phelps, ca. 1880
Silver print
5½ × 3¾ inches

Game in the Adirondacks, 1889
Silver print
6½ × 8½ inches

Echo Camp, Raquette Lake, ca. 1886
Silver print
4¼ × 7¼ inches

Lumber Shanty—Good Story, ca. 1888
Silver print
6½ × 8½ inches

Charcoal Kilns, The Narrows, Chateaugay Lake, 1891
Silver print
6½ × 8½ inches

Drowned Lands of the Lower Raquette, Adirondacks, ca. 1888
Original albumen print
14½ × 18½ inches

Raquette River. At Sweeney Carry, 1888
Silver print
6½ × 8½ inches

Trudeau's Patients Putting on Snowshoes, ca. 1888
Silver print
6½ × 8½ inches

Cottages at Sanitarium, Saranac Lake, ca. 1888
Silver print
6½ × 8½ inches

Unknown Photographers

Two Loggers with Two-Man Saw, ca. 1900
Silver print
3¼ × 5½ inches

Nehasane Train and Firefighters, ca. 1890
Silver print
7 × 9½ inches

Photographs from the Saranac Lake Free Library, Adirondack Collection, Saranac Lake, New York

William L. Distin

Patients on Porch of Childs Infirmary, 1914
Silver print
8 × 10 inches

Dr. and Mrs. Edward Livingston Trudeau and Nurses' Graduating Class, 1914
Silver print
8 × 10 inches

Unknown photographer

New York Hospital for Tuberculosis at Ray Brook, 1920
Silver print
8 × 10 inches

Photographs from the Gordon Stott Collection

J. F. Holley

Dining Room, Camp Stott, ca. 1885
Original albumen print
4½ × 7¾ inches

Seneca Ray Stoddard

Raquette Lake, West from Camp Pine Knot, n. d.
Original albumen print
4½ × 7¾ inches

Illustrations from Periodicals

Julian Rix
Forest Destruction in the Adirondacks— The Effects of Logging and Burning Timber from *Harper's Weekly*, 1/24/1885
Wood engraving on newsprint
11 × 16 inches
The Adirondack Museum, Blue Mountain Lake, New York

Winslow Homer
Trapping in the Adirondacks from *Every Saturday: An Illustrated Journal of Choice Reading;* 12/24/1870
Engraving by J. P. Davis
7 × 9 inches
Peters Collection, The New-York Historical Society

Winslow Homer
Deer Stalking in the Adirondacks in Winter from *Every Saturday: An Illustrated Journal of Choice Reading;* 1/21/1871
7 × 9 inches
Peters Collection, The New-York Historical Society

Winslow Homer
Lumbering in Winter from *Every Saturday: An Illustrated Journal of Choice Reading;* 1/28/1871
Signed by J. P. Davis Sc.
9 × 7 inches
Peters Collection, The New-York Historical Society

Winslow Homer
Camping Out in the Adirondack Mountains from *Harper's Weekly*, 1874
Wood engraving on newsprint
11 × 16 inches
The Adirondack Museum, Blue Mountain Lake, New York

Frederic Remington
Spring Trout Fishing in the Adirondacks— An Odious Comparison of Weights from *Harper's Weekly*, 5/24/1890
Half-tone on newsprint
11 × 16 inches
The Adirondack Museum, Blue Mountain Lake, New York

Frederic Remington
Lumber Camp at Night or Tragedy of the Trees, Part I, from *Collier's Weekly*, 1906
Color reproduction
15 × 10 inches
Thomas Gilcrease Institute of American History and Art, Tulsa, Oklahoma

Frederic Remington
Snaking Logs to the Skidway or Tragedy of the Trees, Part II, from *Collier's Weekly*, 1906
Color reproduction
12 × 9 inches
Thomas Gilcrease Institute of American History and Art, Tulsa, Oklahoma

Frederic Remington
Hauling Logs to the River or Tragedy of the Trees, Part III, from *Collier's Weekly*, 1907
Color reproduction
15 × 10 inches
St. Lawrence University, Owen D. Young Library, Canton, New York

Books

Joel Tyler Headley (Katonah only)
The Adirondacks, or, Life in the Woods
New York: 1849
American Antiquarian Society, Worcester,
Massachusetts

Three steel engravings from *The
Adirondacks:*
R. F. Gignoux—*Lake Henderson*
C. C. Ingham—*Lake Colden*
C. C. Ingham—*Adirondack Pass*
4 × 5 inches
The Adirondack Museum, Blue Mountain
Lake, New York

*Home Book of the Picturesque, or,
American Scenery, Art and Literature*
(Katonah only) with essays by W. Irving,
J. F. Cooper, W. C. Bryant and E. Street
and 13 steel engravings by H. Beckwith
New York: G. P. Putnam, 1852
Gift of James F. Beard
American Antiquarian Society, Worcester,
Massachusetts

William Henry Harrison Murray
(Katonah only)
*Adventures in the Wilderness, or, Camp
Life in the Adirondacks*
Boston: Fields and Osgood & Co., 1869
From the estate of Mary Gage Rice
American Antiquarian Society, Worcester,
Massachusetts

Mildred P. Stokes Hooker
Camp Chronicles VII
Private printing
Private Collection

Seneca Ray Stoddard
Guide Book of 1891
Milo and Ann Williams

Pauline Brandreth (Katonah only)
Sketch Book, ca. 1890-1920
Watercolor on paper
Eleanor B. Wunderlich

Augustus D. Shepard
Camps in the Woods, 1931
Architectural Book Publishing Co., Inc.
Mr. and Mrs. Thad Phillips Collum

Architectural Plans and Drawings

Four Camp Plans from Hale Insurance
Papers
Emerson/Amory Camp
White Pine Camp
Fish Rock Camp
Birch Island Camp
The Adirondack Museum, Blue Mountain
Lake, New York

Augustus D. Shepard
Camp for George H. Storm, Esq., Little
Moose Lake, 1925
Mr. and Mrs. Thad Phillips Collum

Rear Elevation
Blue print
12 × 37 inches

Side Elevation
Blue print
12½ × 37 inches

Front Elevation
Blue print
12 × 38 inches

Site Plan
Blue print
42 × 29 inches

First Floor Plan
Blue print
24 × 40 inches

Augustus D. Shepard
Boathouse for Edward Mallinckrodt,
Little Moose Lake, ca. 1902-1904
The Adirondack Museum, Blue Mountain
Lake, New York

Front Elevation
Blue print
26½ × 16 inches

Side Elevation
Blue print
27½ × 16 inches

Longitudinal Section
Blue print
27 × 16 inches

Furniture

Bureau
Ernest Stowe, ca. 1904
Applied birch bark with yellow birch
trim
72 × 36 × 24 inches
Private Collection

Desk Chair
Ernest Stowe, ca. 1904
Yellow birch
39 inches
Private Collection

Secretary
Ernest Stowe, ca. 1904
Applied white birch bark with yellow
birch trim
70 × 45 × 24 inches
Private Collection

Washstand
Joseph O. A. Bryere, Camp Bright-Side,
Raquette Lake, 1895
Applied birch bark and split twig trim
38 × 32½ × 19 inches
The Adirondack Museum, Blue Mountain
Lake, New York
Gift of Clara O. Bryere

Table
Joseph O. A. Bryere, Camp Bright-Side,
Raquette Lake, 1895
Plain board top with applied birch bark
and lengths of cedar, root base of yellow
birch
31 × 18½ × 25 inches
The Adirondack Museum, Blue Mountain
Lake, New York
Gift of Clara O. Bryere

Table
Paul Maloney, Blue Mountain Lake
A burl on three legged birch root
23 × 18 inches
The Adirondack Museum, Blue Mountain
Lake, New York
Gift of Paul Maloney

Rocking Chair
Long Lake, 1924
Hickory and willow
37½ × 24 inches
The Adirondack Museum, Blue Mountain
Lake, New York
Gift of the Robert Fast Family

Corner Stand
Frank Alger, Eagle Nest, Blue Mountain
Lake, ca. 1935-40
Cedar
74 × 25 × 18 inches
The Adirondack Museum, Blue Mountain
Lake, New York

Deer Foot Gun Rack
38 inches
The Adirondack Museum, Blue Mountain
Lake, New York

Indiana Hickory Child's Chair, ca. 1907
Approx. 25 inches
Private Collection

Indiana Hickory Writing Chair with
folding arms, ca. 1907
Approx. 40 inches
Private Collection

Indiana Hickory Foot Stool, ca. 1907
Approx. 40 inches
Private Collection

Sideboard
Andrew Fisher, Endion, Long Lake, ca.
1890-95
Mosaic twig work
62 × 53 × 17½ inches
Mr. and Mrs. Thomas Bissell

Boats

Adirondack Guideboat, ca. 1950 and Pair
of Oars, ca. 1950
Made by Willard Hanmer, Hanmer Boat
Works, Saranac Lake, New York
Wood with paint
12½ feet long; 37 inch beam
Private Collection

UGO
Canoe made at The Rushton Boat Works,
Canton, New York
White pine/cedar for planking; spruce
root for ribs; cherry or other hardwood
for deck, gunwale and seat
13 feet long; 30 inch beam
Private Collection

Utilitarian Objects

Snowshoes
Wood with rawhide caning
40½ inches long; 10½ inches wide
The Adirondack Museum, Blue Mountain
Lake, New York

Child's Snowshoes
Wood with red woolen decorations
29 inches long; 9½ inches wide
Private Collection

Bear Paw Snowshoes, Grant Boat Shop,
ca. 1900, Boonville, New York
Wood and rawhide
25 inches long; 15 inches wide
The Adirondack Museum, Blue Mountain
Lake, New York

Packbasket
Made by "Indian Joe," Old Forge area,
1920s
20 × 16½ inches
The Adirondack Museum, Blue Mountain
Lake, New York

Packbasket
Woven ash splints, n. d.
13 inches high
The Adirondack Museum, Blue Mountain
Lake, New York

Small Painted Packbasket, n. d.
Milo and Ann Williams

For Logging

Peavey
Iron hook with wooden shaft
48 inches
Private Collection

Peavey
Iron hook with wooden shaft
44 inches long
The Adirondack Museum, Blue Mountain
Lake, New York

Broad Axe (for stripping bark)
Wooden handle 29½ inches; blade
9 inches
Private Collection

Log Marker
Wooden handle with iron stamp
14 inches long
The Adirondack Museum, Blue Mountain
Lake, New York

Log Marker
Wooden handle with iron stamp
16½ inches long
The Adirondack Museum, Blue Mountain
Lake, New York

For Ice Cutting

Ice Tongs
Iron
15 inches
Private Collection

For Trapping

Coyote and Fox Traps
Iron
Each approx. 7 inches long with 12 inch
chains
Private Collection

Conibar Trap (for beaver)
Iron
Private Collection

Otter-skin Stretchers
Wood
Private Collection

Bear Trap
Iron
Private Collection

For Farming

Cranberry Picker
Wooden handle with 14 metal tines from
old pitchfork
13 inches long; 7 inches wide
Private Collection

Scythe
Wooden handle with iron blade
Private Collection

Cowbell
4¾ inches wide; 5½ inches long
Private Collection

For Fishing

Leather Tackle Box
Made by Knickerbocker Cage Co.,
Chicago

Automatic Reel, ca. 1912
Made by Martin Automatic, Ilion, New
York

Bait Casting Reel, 1910
James Heddon's Sons, Dowagiac,
Michigan

First Patented Reel, 1850
"Bird Cage" type by Billinghurst,
Rochester, New York

Fly Rod with Case
Dame Stoddard & Kendall, Boston,
Massachusetts

Yellow Brass Reel, ca. 1870

Orvis Fly Rod, 1892 patent

Long Handled Net

Plug Rod

Book of Flies

All fishing gear from the Hoagy
Carmichael Collection, Croton Falls,
New York

Rustic Cabin Environment

Stuffed Raven, Eight-point Whitetail
Buck (full head mount), Bobcat Skin,
Bear Skull, Bear-paw Snowshoes, Powder
Horn
Private Collection

Stuffed Kingfisher, Stuffed Hawk,
Stuffed Lake Trout, Bearskin, Head Nets,
Rifle
Private Collection

Stove, n. d.
Marked "Van Wormer & McGarvey/
Albany, N. Y."
Cast iron
20½ inches
The Adirondack Museum, Blue Mountain
Lake, New York

Old Creel
Mr. and Mrs. Peter K. Bertine

Tent Platform Environment

Peeled Pole Bed, ca. 1900-1905
Wood
80 × 43½ inches
Kamp Kill Kare

Quilt/Coverlet
Cotton
Mr. and Mrs. John Dillon

Brass Kerosene Heater
Milo and Ann Williams

Burl Table, 1991
Made by Eric Glesmann for the exhibition
30 inches
Mr. and Mrs. Thad Phillips Collum

In the Sculpture Garden

Lean-to (traditional shelter provided by
DEC on public trails)
Peeled pine logs fitted without nails, roof
of cedar shingles, pine flooring
BOCES, Hudson Falls, New York